KW-221-402

FHG
KUPERARD

2008
Recommended
Short Break
Holidays
in Britain & Ireland

Short Break Holidays throughout Britain and Ireland
in Recommended, Registered, or otherwise Approved
Establishments, including Self Catering, Christmas Breaks
and Approved Accommodation all year round
NEW! Haunted Hotels Supplement

hauntedhotelguide.com

ISBN 978-1-85055-396-0

Maps: ©MAPS IN MINUTES™ / Collins Bartholmew 2007

Typeset by FHG Guides Ltd, Paisley.
Printed and bound in Malaysia by Imago.

Distribution. Book Trade: ORCA Book Services, Stanley House,
3 Fleets Lane, Poole, Dorset BH15 3AJ
(Tel: 01202 665432; Fax: 01202 666219)
e-mail: mail@orcabookservices.co.uk
Published by FHG Guides Ltd., Abbey Mill Business Centre,
Seedhill, Paisley PA1 ITJ (Tel: 0141-887 0428 Fax: 0141-889 7204).
e-mail: admin@fhguides.co.uk

Recommended Short Break Holidays is published by FHG Guides Ltd,
part of Kuperard Group.

Cover design: FHG Guides
Cover Pictures: courtesy of Corse Lawn House (full details page 73)
and hauntedhotelguide.com

symbols

 Totally non-smoking   Pets Welcome

 Children Welcome   Christmas Breaks

 Suitable for Disabled Guests   Licensed

Contents

Foreword

A city or country break could be just what's needed to perk you up before the festive season begins, or maybe you'll need a relaxing break to help you wind down when it's all over. Whatever you're looking for, this bright and colourful edition of Recommended Short Breaks with its fine selection of accommodation should give you plenty of choice. There are opportunities for active or relaxing breaks, and accommodation ranges from large hotels with full facilities to B&Bs, self-catering properties and caravans, always popular with children.

If you have a sense of adventure, and are feeling really brave, why not visit one of the hotels in our new **HAUNTED HOTELS** supplement (pages 7-24) where you can choose from a selection of haunted castles, manor houses and hotels. To help you decide we have included a brief history of the ghosts and ghouls to be found in each one.

Whatever your choice, you will find a high level of courtesy and comfort, with friendly and helpful staff, and proprietors who do their best to ensure you have an enjoyable visit. To help you plan your holiday, we have included some useful information on each area, and don't forget to use our Readers' Offer Vouchers (pages 197-204) if you are near any of the attractions which are kindly participating.

Our aim in **RECOMMENDED SHORT BREAK HOLIDAYS** is to include only hotels and other holiday accommodation with an accepted recommendation or rating of some national standing. As publishers, we do not actually inspect or recommend individual advertisers, but all entries have agreed to the principal of inspection by the publisher if this should prove necessary. We show VisitBritain and other gradings where appropriate. It is important to remember, however, that lack of such symbols or gradings may simply mean that the advertiser is waiting to be inspected, or indeed, that he has his own good reasons for feeling that such ratings are not the only measure of good holiday accommodation.

If you've found a particularly recommendable Short Break either here or from another source, please let us know. You might want to keep it to yourself, but a pleasure shared is an extra pleasure gained – sometimes.

Anne Cuthbertson,
Editor

Ratings & Awards

For the first time ever the AA, VisitBritain, VisitScotland, and the Wales Tourist Board will use a single method of assessing and rating serviced accommodation. Irrespective of which organisation inspects an establishment the rating awarded will be the same, using a common set of standards, giving a clear guide of what to expect. The RAC is no longer operating an Hotel inspection and accreditation business.

Accommodation Standards: Star Grading Scheme

Using a scale of 1-5 stars the objective quality ratings give a clear indication of accommodation standard, cleanliness, ambience, hospitality, service and food, This shows the full range of standards suitable for every budget and preference, and allows visitors to distinguish between the quality of accommodation and facilities on offer in different establishments. All types of board and self-catering accommodation are covered, including hotels, B&Bs, holiday parks, campus accommodation, hostels, caravans and camping, and boats.

The more stars, the higher level of quality

★★★★★
exceptional quality, with a degree of luxury

★★★★
excellent standard throughout

★★★
very good level of quality and comfort

★★
good quality, well presented and well run

★
acceptable quality; simple, practical, no frills

VisitBritain and the regional tourist boards, enjoyEngland.com, VisitScotland and VisitWales, and the AA have full details of the grading system on their websites

National Accessible Scheme

If you have particular mobility, visual or hearing needs, look out for the National Accessible Scheme. You can be confident of finding accommodation or attractions that meet your needs by looking for the following symbols.

 Typically suitable for a person with sufficient mobility to climb a flight of steps but would benefit from fixtures and fittings to aid balance

 Typically suitable for a person with restricted walking ability and for those that may need to use a wheelchair some of the time and can negotiate a maximum of three steps

 Typically suitable for a person who depends on the use of a wheelchair and transfers unaided to and from the wheelchair in a seated position. This person may be an independent traveller

 Typically suitable for a person who depends on the use of a wheelchair in a seated position. This person also requires personal or mechanical assistance (eg carer, hoist).

England and Wales · Counties

Unitary Authorities – England & Wales

1. Plymouth	12. Windsor & Maidenhead	23. Milton Keynes	34. Blackpool
2. Torbay	13. Bracknell Forest	24. Peterborough	35. N.E. Lincolnshire
3. Poole	14. Wokingham	25. Leicester	36. North Lincolnshire
4. Bournemouth	15. Reading	26. Nottingham	37. Kingston-upon-Hull
5. Southampton	16. West Berkshire	27. Derby	38. York
6. Portsmouth	17. Swindon	28. Telford & Wrekin	39. Redcar & Cleveland
7. Brighton & Hove	18. Bath & Northeast Somerset	29. Stoke-on-Trent	40. Middlesborough
8. Medway	19. North Somerset	30. Warrington	41. Stockton-on-Tees
9. Thurrock	20. Bristol	31. Halton	42. Darlington
10. Southend	21. South Gloucestershire	32. Merseyside	43. Hartlepool
11. Slough	22. Luton	33. Blackburn with Darwen	

NORTH WALES
a. Denbighshire
b. Flintshire
c. Wrexham

SOUTH WALES
d. Swansea
e. Neath & Port Talbot
f. Bridgend
g. Rhondda Cynon Taff
h. Merthyr Tydfil
i. Vale of Glamorgan
j. Cardiff
k. Caerphilly
l. Blaenau Gwent
m. Torfaen
n. Newport
o. Monmouthshire

hauntedhotelguide.com

For True Believers or Open-minded Sceptics, this supplement gives you the opportunity to visit som of the Most Haunted Hotels in the Country.

Experience the Unexplained!

hauntedhotelguide.com was developed in late 2005 in response to the overwhelming demand for a definitive directory of haunted accommodation throughout the UK. With the public's interest in all things paranormal constantly growing, and with increasingly popular TV shows like "*Most Haunted*", "*Dead Famous*" and "*Derek Acorah's Ghost Towns*" every hotel seems to have a ghost or two to boast about.

Whether you are a hardcore ghost fan or open-minded sceptic, **hauntedhotelguide.com** will provide you with invaluable haunted history about the ghostly goings-on at each hotel, along with the usual information you would expect to find from a regular hotel guide. With around 500 haunted hotels throughout the country, it should be easy to find the perfect location for your stay.

Whilst many other hotel guides concentrate on facilities provided, often the really interesting things, such as where to find the ghost of a servant girl in the Station Hotel or where the bones of the 'Blue Boy' of Chillingham Castle were discovered, are overlooked… Not by us… As you'd expect, we positively encourage reports such as these as we believe that the haunted history of a hotel is just as important as its facilities and we feel that the possibility of seeing a ghost tends to remain etched in your mind much longer than the amount of sherry you received on the welcome tray!

With detailed descriptions and images of the Haunted Hotels and Haunted Inns in this supplement and on our site, **hauntedhotelguide.com** is totally unique: Discover the Green Lady of Comlongon Castle; investigate the presence of a spectral monk in the Tansy Room at Hazlewood Castle, or try and spot the Ghostly Lady Jane in Dalston Hall.

Many of our hotels have been investigated by our Mediums, psychics and paranormal investigators. James Griffiths (*Derek Acorah's Ghost Towns*), one of our mediums, has certainly had a few 'interesting' experiences to say the least:

'Having had the opportunity to visit some of the most haunted hotels throughout the UK, I can honestly say that they do live up to expectations! Being rather rudely pulled out of bed at the dead of night by the poisoned spectre of a lady does leave you wondering whether you will be charged extra for it in the morning as you were sure it wasn't mentioned in the brochure… Finding yourself confronted by a sword-wielding soldier within a castle gate house with only a torch and your mobile phone to defend yourself makes you question your decision to venture out on Halloween! And investigating a hotel in a village renowned for at least 12 ghosts, wondering which one they are all staying at and praying it's not yours, make's you realise there truly is another world waiting to be discovered…'

James Griffiths

This first edition of the **hauntedhotelguide.com** supplement is only a taster as next year, along with FHG guides, we are producing a full 100 page haunted supplement showcasing the most haunted hotels throughout the UK. If you want to find out to find out more about the hotels in this supplement or if you want to discover a haunted hotel near you, take a look at **hauntedhotelguide.com.**

We hope you enjoy the guide and may all your experiences be unexplainable…

The luxurious **Flitwick Manor** is a Georgian gem. If you are fortunate enough, you may witness the ghost of an ex-housekeeper who is said to haunt the corridors...

Nestling in the tranquillity of acres of rolling gardens and wooded parkland, Flitwick Manor is a luxury hotel in the South East of England. This country house hotel, located near Woburn, is a classical Georgian house that continues its ancestral traditions of hospitality.

The cosy lounge of Flitwick Manor is elegantly furnished, providing the perfect retreat for those seeking peace and relaxation.

For private functions or business meetings, this country house hotel offers the ultimate in luxury in the South East, all just one hour from the centre of London.

With two AA rosettes, the restaurant at this luxury hotel is rated as one of the finest in the country and offers the ideal combination of fine dining in a delightful setting.

The 17 individually designed guestrooms and suites, furnished with fine antiques and period pieces, blend effortlessly together to offer guests a comfortable and endearing stay. If you're looking for a luxury hotel in the South East, look no further than Flitwick Manor.

Flitwick Manor

Church Road , Flitwick
Bedfordshire MK45 1AE
Tel: 01525 712242
Email : flitwick@menzieshotels.co.uk
www.menzies-hotels.co.uk

HOTEL FEATURES

- 24 hour room service
- Award-winning restaurant
- Drawing room
- Gardens and woodlands
- Tennis Court • Croquet Lawn
- Helicopter landing pad

Haunted History

hauntedhotelguide.com

Flitwick Manor is reputedly haunted by an ex-housekeeper who, over 100 years ago, was dismissed for allegedly poisoning one of the Lyall family, the former owners of the Manor. After the Old Housekeeper (whose proper name no-one knows) died, it seems her spirit decided to take up residence again at Flitwick.

She keeps herself to herself and doesn't stray much from the bedroom she has made her own. Staff at Flitwick Manor know the housekeeper's favourite chair - she even leaves an impression in the seat after sitting down!

Whilst building work was being carried out on Flitwick Manor, a concealed room was discovered behind some panelling. It has been suggested that this could have been the housekeeper's quarters. Ever since then the spirit has been making herself known to guests throughout the hotel. One guest was woken to find her sitting on the end of his bed, and a duty manager witnessed the ghost in one of the corridors…

The stunning 16th Century **Lion and Swan Inn** in Congleton is steeped in history... A dark haired female spirit said to have lived during the Middle Ages often makes an appearance...

Situated at the heart of the attractive market town of Congleton, the strikingly timbered Lion and Swan Hotel is a traditional coaching inn which boasts 21 attractive bedrooms with every modern amenity, a first class restaurant which prides itself on a high standard of cuisine, and a friendly bar which is open to residents and non residents alike featuring a wide selection of real ales, lagers, wines & spirits..

Our restaurant, open for Breakfast, Lunch and Dinner seven days a week, serves an eclectic selection of dishes freshly prepared in house using locally sourced fresh ingredients. The fireplace in the restaurant is a particular delight and source of mystery with its complex and intriguing carvings...

Lion & Swan Hotel

Swan Bank, Congleton, Cheshire
Tel: 01260 273 115
Email: info@lionandswan.co.uk
www.lionandswan.co.uk

HOTEL FEATURES
- Remote Control Colour Television
  - AM/FM radio alarm clock
  - Hairdryer • Ironing Facilities
    - Full tea and coffee making facilities.

Haunted History   **haunted**hotelguide .com

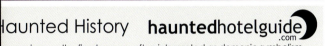

The carvings on the fireplace are often interpreted as demonic symbolism. This may have something to do with the **Lion and Swan's** ghost - a young, brown haired woman, who often appears around a new moon, wearing nothing but a pair of clogs and a smile!

This young spirit reputedly dates back to the Middle Ages. It is alleged that she was unable to conceive and drank a potion to aid conception. However, instead of creating new life, the potion took hers. She has been seen on many occasions tending the fire beneath the carved fireplace...

The Tudor Suite is also renowned for its mysterious goings on. It sometimes has a cold atmosphere, and most of the unexplained noises emanate from here at night.

The **George and Dragon Hotel** in Chester is an imposing building situated just outside the city walls. As Chester is one of the most haunted cities in the UK, it is no surprise that this hotel has its own ghosts as guests...

A short walk from Chester City centre, the George and Dragon is a traditional hostelry that blends well with a modern lively bar. Our open plan lounge, with three fireplaces, creates a warm and cosy atmosphere to enjoy our well stocked cellar and traditional food. The character building which now stands on the site is around 100 years old, but there has been a public house or coaching inn, of some kind, on the site for a lot longer.

There is also believed to be a burial ground of Roman origin on the site, which is possible given that Chester, or Dewa was an important Roman town.

George & Dragon

1 Liverpool Road
Chester, Cheshire CH2 1AA
Tel: 01244 380714
Email : 7783@greeneking.co.uk
www.oldenglishinns.co.uk

HOTEL FEATURES
- Hairdryer
- Iron & Ironing Board
- Tea/Coffee • TV
- All en suite with shower room

Haunted History   **haunted**hotelguide .com

Chester boasts over 2000 years of documented history. Its crypts, narrow streets and alley ways play host to many infamous ghosts and spirits and the **George and Dragon Hotel** is no exception. This hotel is reputedly haunted by a legion of Roman soldiers.

The George and Dragon is situated on the site of the old Roman road leading out from Chester. Roman military law forbade the burial of soldiers within the city walls of Dewa and so many were buried immediately outside and some could quite feasibly be buried beneath the hotel.

Over the centuries the sound of marching feet beneath the floors has been heard by staff and guests alike. Strangely, the sound seems loudest in the cellars, which would have been closer to the original Roman ground level...

Dalston Hall is a luxurious 15th Century Mansion with a fascinating history. Lady Jane is said to appear in Tudor dress in the gallery above the manorial hall. Other ghosts include a Handyman, 'Sad Emily' and a Young Girl...

Guests can expect a venue with a difference, and as witnessed by the GMTV 'Haunted' team, a few ghosts! The hotel offers a peaceful and tranquil setting to guests, and the perfect retreat in the beautiful countryside on the northern edge of the Lake District, ideally placed for the national treasure Hadrian's Wall.

The hotel has recently undergone considerable refurbishment involving the ground floor public areas being restyled but still keeping the original character of this 15th Century family Mansion. The bedrooms have also been restyled to an elegant character but each has their own unique luxurious style.

Dalston Hall

Carlisle
Cumbria CA5 7JX
Tel: +44 (0)1228 710271
Email: enquiries@dalstonhall.com
www.dalston-hall-hotel.co.uk

HOTEL FEATURES

- En suite bathroom
- Tea & Coffee making facilities
- TV • Award Winning Restaurant
- Wedding Licence
- Conference Facilities

Haunted History **haunted**hotelguide
.com

Dalston Hall plays host to many ghosts, the first of which, the spirit of a Victorian handyman, has been seen wandering the grounds. In the Baronial Hall you may find Dalston Hall's oldest ghost – known to the staff as Lady Jane. She appears in Tudor dress and may well be a member of one of the Dalston families who owned the Hall for such a long time.

The cellars of the hotel are haunted by the sinister Mr Fingernails and many of the bedrooms are reputed to have spectral guests: Room 4 is said to be haunted by a poor maid who threw herself from the Pele tower and in Room 12 guests have complained of being woken by girls' voices whispering…

Set in 18 acres, **Walworth Castle** is one of the country 's finest historic hotels, parts of which date back to the 12th century

Walworth Castle Hotel just outside Darlington in County Durham, was built in 1189 and is one of the few castle hotels in England. Recently refurbished to an extremely high standard by owners Rachel and Chris Swain, Walworth Castle Hotel really is the ideal venue to sample England's Living History

Each of the 34 bedrooms and numerous reception rooms has its own particular character many with individually designed upholstery. The feature rooms have been recently refurbished to an extremely high standard Walworth Castle boasts two fabulous restaurants (one award-winning) and a traditional 'pub'. The choice of hospitality at Walworth Castle Hotel really is second to none.

Walworth Castle

Walworth, Darlington
Durham DL2 2LY
Tel: +44 (0)1325 485470
Email:
enquiries@walworthcastle.co.uk
www.walworthcastle.co.uk

HOTEL FEATURES

- Four-Poster Beds
- Sumptuous Furnishings
- Castle Gardens
- Fabulous Views
- TV

Haunted History **haunted**hotelguide
.com

According to legend, the Lord of the Manor was having an affair with one of the servant girls. Unfortunately, for both parties, the maid fell pregnant. Realising that it would be a great disgrace to his family to father a child with a servant he decided to take drastic action. At the time of the affair, the castle was being renovated so the Lord of the Manor decided to seize the opportunity and had the maid walled up inside a spiral staircase.

It is alleged that she can still be heard climbing the staircase behind the library leading to the turrets of **Walworth Castle**

Other ghostly apparitions at the castle include the spectral replay of a brother's feud resulting in one killing the other, the horse buried in the gardens and the running boy in the corridors...

the stunningly beautiful Redworth Hall dates back to 1744. Redworth was the site of many battles during the Civil War and it appears that some of the soldiers killed in battle are still lingering...

Redworth Hall Hotel is a breathtaking Jacobean country house in County Durham. You'll feel as if you're in the middle of nowhere here as you survey the captivating, landscaped gardens and enchanting woodland. From the moment you sweep up the long driveway to the hotel, you know you're in for a treat. You can enjoy the escapism of this picture postcard setting and within 5 minutes be heading towards Newcastle, historic Durham or York.

This original building still retains many of its original features including an ornate staircase, the Great Hall and several four-poster bedrooms. The Hall also boasts two award winning restaurants and a leisure club.

Aside from the hotel itself, you'll find it's the charm and hospitality of north-east folk at Redworth Hall that will make your stay an incredible one.

Redworth Hall
Redworth,
Durham DL5 6NL
Tel: +44 (0)1388 770 600
Email:
redworthhall@paramount-hotels.co.uk
www.paramount-redworthhall.co.uk

HOTEL FEATURES
- Concierge
- Currency exchange
- Safety Deposit Boxes
- Restaurant
- Lounge / Bar
- Barber / Beauty Services

Haunted History

hauntedhotelguide.com

Redworth Hall has a fantastic haunted history and boasts at least two ghosts...

The first is that of a woman who, it appears, felt the urge to throw herself from the top of the Jacobean Tower after her lover left her. She is said to walk the corridors and rooms at the front of the Hall, particularly the bedrooms.

The second ghost relates to one of the former owners of the Hall, Lord Surtee. One of the Lord's many children was 'ill of mind' and his unique way of coping with this was to chain the child up to one of the Great Hall's Fireplaces... day & night . The laughter and crying of young children is sometimes heard in this area of the Great Hall.

Enjoy your stay!

Beautiful **Elvey Farm** dates back to the early 15th Century. This small country hotel is situated in Pluckley, the Most Haunted Village in England, and is renowned for its Ghostly Guests...

Elvey Farm is a medieval farmstead in the village of Pluckley, Kent. The Hall House was built in 1430 and little has changed since then. Once used as a 75 acre farm for cereals and sheep, Elvey is now run as a small country hotel. Guests stay in the converted stable block and barn, and enjoy brand new contemporary bathrooms and excellent personal service, with glorious views over the Kent countryside.

Whether you're sipping champagne on the veranda outside your suite, or you're riding your own horse through our excellent bridleways, you'll be surrounded by the quietest, the prettiest and the most idyllic countryside in Kent.

At breakfast you have fresh eggs from our own chickens, sausages from local farms, tomatoes and fried potatoes from our own gardens. In the evenings, you can sample wine or cider from Kent's vineyards, and admire crafts from local artists. Elvey has been run by local people for centuries. That's why we say Elvey is Kentish to the core.

Elvey Farm

Elvey Lane , Pluckley
KENT TN27 0SU
Tel: 01233 840 442
Email:
bookings@elveyfarm.co.uk
www.elveyfarm.co.uk

HOTEL FEATURES

• Double rooms in the converted stables
• Brand new contemporary
en-suite bathrooms
• Stunning views across the fields.
• A beautiful Dining Room with low beams
• Roaring log fire
• Fabulous Full English Breakfast

Haunted History

According to the Guinness Book of Records, Pluckley is the most haunted village in England. There have been numerous sightings – and at last count, there are 42 Ghosts in the village alone.

Elvey Farm has long been known as the only haunted hotel in the area. Edward Brett, a farmer at Elvey, is reputed to have shot himself here. He may have died over a hundred years ago, but many say Edward is still here. The previous owners of the farm saw Mr Brett on many occasions walking the corridors at night. Many guests have seen him too... Some say he is so vivid, it's as though he's alive today. Guests have reported a strange smell, resembling burning hay. There have been reports of a poltergeist – and paranormal investigators have confirmed the farm is bristling with activity. The present owners have already experienced Edward Brett – his voice has twice been heard whispering in the old dairy where he shot himself.

Many people come to Pluckley to find the ghosts – many people descend on Elvey Farm. At Hallowe'en, the whole village is packed. But there's far more than a ghost here. It's an idyllic location, surrounded by fields, orchards and hop gardens. It's Kent at its best – ghosts and all...

The **Ffolkes Arms** at Hillington is a friendly family run hotel which offers first class accommodation and a wide range of services and facilities. It holds a dark secret however, as it is reputedly haunted by a young nanny who committed suicide…

The hotel, which bears the name of the Ffolkes family, was constructed over three hundred years ago and became well known as a very popular Coaching Inn, being located on the main mailing route from the Midlands in to Norwich. For a period of time the attic rooms of the hotel were used as an overnight gaol for the prison carriages on their way to the prison in Norwich. This now provides the hotel with 20 bedrooms, all tastefully furnished, and complete with en-suite facilities. The rooms also ensure added comfort; each having twin or double beds, remote control colour television, direct dial telephone, tea making facilities, hair dryer and trouser press.

Haunted History   hauntedhotelguide.com

The **Ffolkes Arms** is reputedly haunted by a young nanny, who apparently threw herself out of one of the attic bedrooms during the latter part of the 19th century and was, quite gruesomely, embedded on the iron railings which then ran along the front of the inn.

Her benign spirit is known to wander the bedrooms and corridors of this beautiful hotel.

Ffolkes Arms Hotel
Lynn Road, Hillington,
King's Lynn,
Norfolk, PE31 6BJ
www.ffolkes-arms-hotel.co.uk

HOTEL FEATURES
- En suite facilities
- Television
- Direct Dial Telephone
- Tea and Coffee Making Facilities
- Hair Dryer

The **Schooner Hotel**, situated in Alnmouth, Northumberland has been twice awarded the title of The Most Haunted Hotel in Great Britain and is reputed to have over 60 individual ghosts...

The Famous Schooner Hotel and Restaurant, a Listed 17th century coaching Inn only 100 yards from the beach, river and golf course, has been the hub of Alnmouth village since its first customer back in the 1600's, and remains one of the most well known and respected hotels in the North East of England. Notable persons said to have stayed at The Schooner include Charles Dickens, John Wesley, Basil Rathbone, Douglas Bader and even King George VI and there is always the chance of meeting our Resident Ghost - "Parson Smyth"! There is little doubting that our motto "Comfort with Character" is justly deserved, and this can be seen by the number of guests who return to the Famous Schooner time and time again.

Haunted History   hauntedhotelguide.com

The **Schooner Hotel** has been twice awarded the title of The Most Haunted Hotel in Great Britain by The Poltergeist Society and is reputed to have over 60 individual ghosts. The hotel has a somewhat unclear history, but there are reports of suicides, murders and even of babies being thrown into the fire. It is a very 'active' hotel with over 3000 recent sightings, ranging from ghosts dressed in military uniform to apparitions of a little boy. The sound of screaming, whispers and knocking are also a very common occurrence and are regularly experienced by staff and guests alike.

Schooner Hotel
Alnmouth, Alnwick
Northumberland NE66 2RS
Tel: +44 (0)1665 830216
Email: info@theschoonerhotel.co.uk
www.theschoonerhotel.co.uk

HOTEL FEATURES
- En suite facilities
- Television
- Tea and coffee making facilities
- Licensed Bar & Restaurant
- Conference Facilities

Chillingham Castle

Chillingham, Alnwick
Northumberland NE66 5NJ
Tel: +44 (0)1668 215359
Email:
enquiries@chillingham-castle.com
www.chillingham-castle.com

HOTEL FEATURES

- Colour television, microwave, fridge and electric cooker
- Stunning Grounds
- Log burning stoves
- Logs and kindling for fires

Stunning **Chillingham Castle** with its alarming dungeons and torture chamber has, since the twelve-hundreds, been continuously owned by the family of the Earls Grey and their relations. The Castle is also home to a number a ghosts, the most famous being the 'Blue Boy'...

In a glorious and secluded setting in Northumberland's famously beautiful countryside, Chillingham Castle offers holidaymakers the unbelievable experience of staying in a medieval fortress.

Parts of the Castle and the coach house have been converted into comfortable holiday apartments, offering the opportunity for a memorable holiday.

The extensive grounds are accessible to holiday makers. Within a few miles of the coast and being in close proximity to several golf courses, Chillingham is ideally situated for a unique holiday, with fishing, golf and stately home visits.

Haunted History   **haunted**hotelguide
.com

We have a number of ghosts at **Chillingham Castle**. The most famous is the "Blue Boy" whose moans are often heard around midnight. These noises have been traced to a spot near a passage cut through a ten foot wall, behind which the bones of a young boy and fragments of blue clothing were discovered! People sleeping in that room even today, have been known to see the figure of a young boy dressed in blue, and surrounded by light.

Another ghost, Lady Mary Berkeley, searches for her husband who ran off with her sister. Lady Mary, desolate and broken hearted, lived in the castle by herself with only her baby daughter as a companion. The rustle of her dress can be heard as she passes people by...

The George Hotel

High Street, Dorchester-on-Thames
Oxfordshire OX10 7HH
Tel: 01865 340404
E-mail: info@thegeorgedorch-ester.co.uk
www.thegeorgedorchester.co.uk

HOTEL FEATURES

- En suite bathroom
- Colour TV • Alarm clock Radio
- Direct Dial Telephone
- Cathedral or garden views
- Tea & coffee making facilities

The **George Hotel** is a fifteenth century coaching inn set in the heart of Oxfordshire. In the days of the stagecoach it provided a welcome haven for many an aristocrat including the first Duchess of Marlborough, Sarah Churchill. However, in more recent times we have seen famous guests of a different hue such as author DH Lawrence.

The Buildings of The George Hotel have changed little since their heyday as a coaching inn. It retains all the beauty and charm of those days whilst offering every modern amenity.

The Hotel provides 17 en-suite bedrooms set in peaceful surroundings; all individually decorated and furnished with fine antiques. Our owners have created a décor which suits the requirements of modern times and facilities whilst maintaining the spirit of the past.

Haunted History   **haunted**hotelguide
.com

This beautiful hotel is directly opposite Dorchester Abbey and is well renowned for its spectral visitors. Being so close to the Abbey it is little surprise that a mischievous monk often frequents Room 6. The spirit of an old lady has also been 'picked up' by a number of mediums. She is present in Room 3 of the hotel and on occasion, her reflection has been seen through the windows.

Another visitor to the **George Hotel** frequents one of the bedrooms in particular – The Vicar's Room. This room is reputed to be haunted by a ghost of a sad-looking girl dressed in a white gown.

The beautiful **Bull Hotel** at Long Melford dates back to the Fifteenth Century. The Ghost of Richard Evered, murdered there in 1648, still roams the Hotel... Its original timber work, both outside and inside is unusually well preserved. That of the exterior was discovered in 1935 when a hundred year old brick front was removed. On a beam in the lounge is carved a 'Wildman' or 'Woodwose', a mysterious being frequently depicted in the decoration of the middle ages, reputedly to ward off evil spirits.

The Bull Hotel, boasting 25 en-suite bedrooms, was tastefully refurbished in 2003 and is renowned for its excellent cuisine and chef's specialities...

Haunted History   **haunted**hotelguide_{.com}

The **Bull Hotel** is quite famous for its ghosts. Indeed it is mentioned in a number of books on the subject. According to the legend, a man named "Richard Evered" was murdered there in 1648. The crime had a strange twist however, as the victim's body disappeared overnight! It is said that the spirit of Richard Evered roams the Bull Hotel now.

Along with a number of apparitions, the Bull is also known for its poltergeist activity: a large oak door opens and closes by itself; chairs move around the dining room of their own accord and the sound of breaking crockery has been heard by several guests. One person even had a copper jug thrown at them.

It's definitely a place we would recommend!

Bull Hotel

Hall Street, Long Melford
Sudbury, Suffolk CO10 9JG
Tel: 01787 378494
Email:
bull.longmelford@greeneking.co.uk
www.thebull-hotel.com

HOTEL FEATURES

- Colour Television
- Mini Stereo
- Direct Dial Telephones
- Ironing Boards • Irons •Hairdryers
- Tea & coffee making facilities

Steeped in history **Brownsover Hall** is now a fabulous hotel. It is said to be haunted by One Handed Boughton - a former inhabitant of the hall who lost his arm during Elizabethan times...

The Hall Hotel is a Grade 11 Listed Victorian Gothic mansion nestling in 7 acres of woodland and garden. This magnificent building has a dramatic interior with sweeping staircase and crackling log fires. With rich colours and plenty of character and charm the Brownsover Hall Hotel has a distinct unique charm. The Hall borders three counties, making it the ideal base for visiting Warwick, Stratford-upon-Avon and the North Cotswolds.

Haunted History   **haunted**hotelguide_{.com}

A member of the Boughton-Leigh family, who had his hand severed at the time of Queen Elizabeth I, is reputed to haunt **Brownsover Hall** despite many attempts to exorcise the ghost. The spirit was finally imprisoned in a glass bottle and thrown into a nearby lake. Everything was fine at the Hall until the bottle was discovered by a group of fishermen and returned to the Hall around 100 years ago...

The spirit of One-handed Boughton, as he was known, is reputed to haunt the grounds, and many unexplained noises, footsteps and voices can often be heard emanating from the tower...

Brownsover Hall

Brownsover Lane, Old Brownsover
Rugby,Warwickshire CV21 1HU
Tel: +44 (0)1788 546100
Email:
gm.brownsoverhall@foliohotels.com
www.foliohotels.com/brownsoverhall

HOTEL FEATURES

- Gilbert Scott Restaurant
- Warwick Bar
- WiFi internet access
- Nearest Rail Link: Rugby 1mile
- Nearest Airport: Birmingham

Built in 1220 and reputed to be the oldest purpose built hotel in England, The **Old Bell Hotel** is still offering quintessentially English warmth, comfort and hospitality nearly eight hundred years later.

Standing alongside Malmesbury's medieval Abbey, in England's first capital, the hotel provides outstanding levels of service and retains the ambience of a bygone age.

There are 31 en suite bedrooms, 15 in the main house , each furnished in an individual style, some with antique furniture, and a further 16 in the Coach House

The Old Bell Hotel

Abbey Row, Malmesbury
Wiltshire SN16 0AG
Tel: 01666 822344
Email:
www.oldbellhotel.com

HOTEL FEATURES

- En Suite Facilities
- Televisions with integral
- DVD players, Sky TV
- Wired broadband internet access.

Haunted History   hauntedhotelguide.com

The **Old Bell Hotel** is renowned for its mysterious goings on - which is not surprising as the east wing of the hotel is built directly on part of the former abbey.

The hotel's most famous ghost is said to be the spirit of a lady who was unhappily married in the abbey. Her ghost, known as the Grey Lady, has reputedly been seen wandering about the bedrooms, in particular the James Ody Room.

Many more strange happenings have occurred at the Old Bell including glasses rising into the air and smashing by themselves in the Danvers Room; wardrobes mysteriously jamming themselves against doors in the Foe Room and night porters reporting a cold atmosphere when walking down the corridor towards the Salon…

Could these experiences all be attributed to the Grey Lady… or are there more mischievous spirits at the Old Bell?

The **Station Hotel,** originally built in the early 20th Century has played host to many famous guests, including Bob Hope and Laurel and Hardy. The spirit of a girl murdered in the hotel is said to roam the corridors...

The Station Hotel offers a warm and friendly atmosphere. Set in the heart of the Midlands, the hotel is easily accessible from Junction 2 of the M5 which is only five minutes drive away.

Originally built in 1910, The Station was demolished in 1936 in order to build a larger hotel. This became particularly popular with theatrical artists playing the Hippodrome Theatre, once situated opposite. Laurel & Hardy, Bob Hope, Bing Crosby and George Formby are amongst the famous names that have stayed at this historic Hotel.

Station Hotel

Castle Hill, Dudley
West Midlands DY1 4RA
Tel: +44 (0)1384 253418
Email:
sales@stationhoteldudley.co.uk
www.stationhoteldudley.co.uk

HOTEL FEATURES

- En suite bathroom
- Colour TV
- Radio
- Tea & Coffee Making Facilities
- Wedding Facilities

Haunted History   hauntedhotelguide.com

Going back to the beginning, researching the building was almost impossible due to the misplacement of many archive records. However, it is up to you to decide whether the folklore stories told about the hotel over the years are true or not.....

The story tells of a hotel manager who enticed a servant girl into the cellar. Spurning his advances and threatening to tell his wife, the girl was murdered by the hotel manager. He strangled and stabbed her then hid her body in a barrel. 'Most Haunted's Derek Acorah 'picked up' the ghost of the murdered girl as well as the spirit of writer George Lawley and the spirits of two young children. The other, as yet unnamed spirit Acorah picked up on, is rumoured to be sitting waiting for someone in the infamous ROOM 214.

...unning **Hazlewood Castle** is steeped in history and was ...st mentioned in the Doomsday Book carried out for King ...Villiam. Ghostly apparitions and sounds are regularly ...xperienced...

...et in seventy-seven acres of tranquil parkland Hazlewood ...astle, a former monastery and retreat has been ...houghtfully and tastefully designed to offer a distinctly ...ifferent lifestyle experience. Hazlewood combines the ...egance of the Castle with the excellence of the food ...nd service offered to all our guests. Whether visiting ...azlewood for the first time with friends or as a delegate at ...he of our major conferences you will always be greeted ...ith a warm welcome. We have twenty-one bedrooms ...nd suites at Hazlewood. Nine of them are situated in the ...ain castle and twelve are in our annex area "St ...argaret's" which is located in our picturesque Courtyard. ...l bedrooms are beautifully decorated to the highest ...andards, with great care taken to enhance their natural ...eauty. All bedrooms are individual and vary in shape and ...res, designed to provide a relaxing haven full of ...hickknacks (and little rubber ducks!).

Hazlewood Castle

Paradise Lane, Hazlewood
Tadcaster
North Yorkshire LS24 9NJ
Tel: 01937 535353
Email: info@hazlewood-castle.co.uk
www.hazlewood-castle.co.uk

HOTEL FEATURES

- Beautiful Restaurant
- Weddings
- Satellite television
- Tea and Coffee making Facilities
- Modem Links for E-mail and Internet Access
- En suite Bathrooms

Haunted History

hauntedhotelguide.com

Hazlewood Castle is steeped in history and it is no surprise that it has its fair share of ghosts.
Many of the bedrooms throughout the hotel are haunted. Tansy bedroom, for example, is mentioned in a ghost book as having a monk dressed in black 'making his presence felt' in the room.
Staff and guests alike have seen and felt strange presences in Lavender bedroom, Rose Bedroom and the Jasmine Suite.
Downstairs in the hotel, a priest has been seen walking from the direction of the Great Hall into the Library and then disappear. As the castle was a former monastery, the monks and priests would walk from the Great Hall to the Tower to go down into the cloisters, which is where the fireplace is now positioned in the Library
Voices have also been heard at Hazlewood Castle... A voice saying "goodnight" was heard by a chef as she was leaving the Restaurant Anise to enter Reception but no-one was there, and over the Christmas period of 2003 one guest complained repeatedly overnight of a baby crying keeping her awake. However, no babies were in the adjoining rooms.

Beautiful **Mosborough Hall** dates back hundreds of years and is steeped in history. It is now a luxurious hotel and is also home to a number of ghosts, including the White Lady and a Spectral Dog...

A wealth of quality, service and history wait for you at Mosborough Hall Hotel. The Hotel was lovingly restored in 1974 from a magnificent 750 year old Manor House. No expense has been spared, with each room having been carefully restored and decorated to retain the historic ambience that is rarely enjoyed today. An ancient doorway leads from the friendly reception to the oak bar, with minstrel gallery and old stone mullioned windows, inviting you to relax in comfort as you take a drink, perhaps before enjoying the superb cuisine for which the restaurant has been long celebrated. The Restaurant consistently maintains its Rosettes award-winning standard with fresh home made breads, chocolates and patisseries.

Mosborough Hall has a selection of 47 rooms to cover all tastes; from Four Poster Feature Rooms with authentic wall panelling for that special occasion, to recently renovated Contemporary Rooms.

Mosborough Hall

High Street, Mosborough
Sheffield
South Yorkshire S20 5EA
Tel: 0114 248 4353
Email: hotel@mosboroughhall.co.uk
www.mosboroughhall.co.uk

HOTEL FEATURES

- Beautiful Award-winning Restaurant
- Weddings
- Conference Facilities
- Satellite Television
- Tea and Coffee making Facilities
- Telephone Modem Links
for E-mail and Internet Access

Haunted History

hauntedhotelguide.com

Mosborough Hall was an ancient Manor House, the earliest parts of which date back to medieval times. It survives today as Mosborough Hall Hotel and still retains its stately charm behind a somewhat foreboding exterior appearance. Partly hidden by tall, stark trees, an air of mystery is enhanced by a high stone wall which hides the intimacies of the Hall from passers-by using the quiet Hallow Lane. There was a doorway through the wall, which was used by servants when they collected milk or eggs from the farm opposite. Many tales were told of strange noises and voices heard around this doorway, sufficient enough to raise a prickle on the back of the neck when walking past in the dim light of a fading evening.

Stories of a doctor waking up in his bed dripping with blood, a spectral dog and The White Lady of Mosborough Hall are enough to make the blood run cold. The White Lady, thought to have been a governess at the hotel killed by the squire with whom she was in love, is regularly seen throughout the hotel.

eautiful **Comlongon Castle** dates back to the 1300s. his truly breathtaking building is now a luxurious hotel. he hotel also boasts a ghost - that of the 'Green ady', thought to be the spirit of Marion Carruthers... omlongon Castle, near Gretna in Scotland, is a estored 14th Century Medieval Scottish Castle /edding Venue and luxurious Baronial Hotel with 14 dividually themed luxury en-suite 4-poster bedrooms. he wedding castle hotel has two Oak panelled estaurants for receptions and a private residents' bar. ur chefs specialise in local produce, changing their enus daily.

his Romantic Medieval Castle is the perfect wedding enue for your wedding castle reception or elebration in Scotland. Steeped in Scottish Border story, Comlongon Castle is more than just fantastic otel – it has fantastic displays of armour, weapons and anners, whilst the opulent bedrooms boast 4-poster eds and jacuzzis providing a stunning blend of edieval and modern luxury.

Comlongon Castle

Clarencefield , Dumfries
Dumfries and Galloway DG1 4NA
Tel: 01387 870283
Email:
reception@comlongon.co.uk
www.comlongon.com

HOTEL FEATURES

- Four-Poster Suites
- En suite Facilities
- Breathtaking Surroundings
- Jacuzzi Baths

Haunted History

hauntedhotelguide.com

Marion Carruthers is a presence that has been felt within **Comlongon Castle** for over four centuries. Since her death in 1570 there have been numerous sightings of a "Green Lady" wandering the grounds of the estate. The smell of apples often precedes these apparitions.

Over the last decade sightings have been concentrated upon one room in particular. Guests have reported numerous sightings of a figure in a long dress either sitting on the four-poster bed or drifting between the bed and door. Most stories from guests mention the moving of jewellery, particularly watches and bracelets, from one location to another.

Sightings at one period numbered almost once a month, so much so that staff began to talk of the suite as "Marion's room". Upon the introduction of new jacuzzis in several rooms, including Marion's, it seemed the obvious choice to name this as the Carruthers suite.

If you wish to book this room please inform reception. We are always interested in information you gather...

Ardoe House Hotel

South Deeside Road, Blairs
Aberdeen AB12 5YP
Tel: 01224 860 600
Email: H6626@accor.com
www.mercure.com

HOTEL FEATURES
- 24 hour room service
- Satellite Television
- Tea and Coffee making Facilities
- Swimming Pool
- State of the Art Beauty Salon

Ardoe House dates back to 1878. The hotel's traditional decor including wood panelled walls, enormous fireplaces and a grand staircase are not the only reminders of its past - some of the hotel's previous inhabitants still remain. Ardoe House is a luxurious modern hotel, beautifully crafted from an imposing 19th century mansion house and inspired by the royal residence of Balmoral Castle, a few miles upstream.

Throwing open your window to capture the morning light as it spills over the River Dee is one of the pure delights of a stay at the Ardoe House. We've created over one hundred bedrooms in this historic setting, each one capturing the distinctly romantic mood of the surrounding countryside. Depending on your mood you can choose to dine in our elegant AA rosette winning restaurant or enjoy a meal in the relaxed surroundings of the Laird's Bar, where you can enjoy a dram in front of a crackling fire in Winter.
It is, quite simply, beautiful.

Haunted History   hauntedhotelguide.com

Ardoe House is no stranger to mysterious noises and ghostly apparitions. The hotel is said to be haunted by the white lady, thought to be Katherine Ogston, the wife of soap merchant Alexander Milne Ogston. Her spirit has been seen throughout the hotel but most of the 'activity' seems to centre round a portrait of Katherine on the main stairs.

There are conflicting reports as to who this ghost is. Whilst some maintain that the White Lady is the spirit of Katherine Ogston, others believe that the ghost is the spirit of the daughter of a former owner who committed suicide…

Maesmawr Hall Hotel

Caersws, Powys, SY17 5SF.
Tel: 01686 688255
Fax: 01686 688410
Email:
information@maesmawr.co.uk
www.maesmawr.co.uk

HOTEL FEATURES
- En suite rooms
- Stunning Views
- Welsh Coastline and attractions nearby

Maesmawr Hall Hotel, Caersws is situated in the beautiful valley of the Severn. This stunning period house is privately owned and personally supervised by the resident proprietors, Tim and Matthew Lewis.

The hotel is one of the most complete and picturesque of the old half-timbered houses of Montgomeryshire and a fine example of the central chimney timber-framed houses which are characteristic of Mid Wales. The general appearance of the house suggests a mid 17th Century dwelling but it has been established that the house was in existence before 1600. The hotel has 17 en-suite bedrooms with modern facilities, many of which have been recently refurbished to a high standard and offer stunning views over the grounds and the breathtaking countryside beyond

Whether it's simply an overnight stay with bed and breakfast, or a longer holiday, Maesmawr Hall combines the quiet tranquillity of a country house with the atmosphere of a popular venue.

Haunted History   hauntedhotelguide.com

All old houses with the slightest self respect claim to possess a ghost and **Maesmawr Hall** is no exception! The Grey Lady, an unknown spectre and Robin Drwg (Wicked Robin), assuming the form of a bull, are said to roam the Hall.

Robin Drwg was a renowned rapscallion in his day and it appears that he caused much mischief and alarm to those who encountered him. He was eventually overcome by the efforts of seven parsons of undoubted ability and laid in Llyn Tarw (the Bull's Pool)….

Whether the endeavours of the worthy gentlemen were successful or not is a matter of conjecture, but it is claimed that his half man/half beastly form still lurks!

Ruthin Castle (the "Red Fort") originally dates from before 1277 and dominates the historic Welsh rural market town of Ruthin. The infamous Grey Lady is a regular visitor to this beautiful hotel...

Ruthin Castle's wood panelled entrance hall is warmly lit and several of the inner rooms have the added warmth of beautifully carved stone and wood fireplaces with open fires that make them cosy despite their scale. Original oil paintings line the Inner Hallway and are to be found in several of the public rooms. The castle has a proud, centuries-old tradition of providing hospitality and comfort, including hosting numerous Royal guests. It is difficult not just to feel welcome here but also to feel part of the great history of the castle and those that have come before. The Castle boasts 62 individually designed bedrooms. Most of the rooms enjoy views over the 30 acres of gardens, parkland and woods of the estate and towards the surrounding Welsh countryside. Many rooms have four-poster beds and original fireplaces (currently not in use) and most have original antique pieces of furniture.

Ruthin Castle

Ruthin
Denbighshire LL15 2NU
Tel: 01824 702664
Email:
reception@ruthincastle.co.uk
www.ruthincastle.co.uk

HOTEL FEATURES

- Fully equipped Gym
- Award-winning Restaurant
- Hairdryer, bath and/or shower
- Remote control colour television
- Beautiful Grounds
- Hospitality Beverages

Haunted History

hauntedhotelguide.com

There are endless tales of hauntings in and around the castle. However there is a lot of historic evidence which gives the rumours credence and many believe them to be true.

The castle ghost is known as the 'Grey Lady' as she is dressed from head to foot in grey. One of the most popular explanations as to who this spirit may be is that she was the wife of the second in command at the castle when it was 'the Red Fort' and was first inhabited by the armies of Edward I. The story goes that the 'Grey Lady' discovered that her husband, a powerful man, was having an affair and took it upon herself to murder his lover with an axe! Once this heinous crime was discovered, the 'Grey Lady' was arrested and sentenced to death. However, she was buried outside the walls of the Castle so as not to bury her on consecrated ground. Her grave can still be seen today, as can her spirit wandering around the battlements of the Castle.

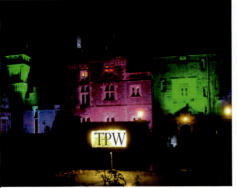

Craig-y-Nos Castle nestles in the lovely Upper Swansea Valley next to the River Tawe. The castle was the former home of opera diva, Adelina Patti and is now a beautiful hotel with a very haunted history...

Craig-y-nos Castle is situated in an area of outstanding natural beauty. With its wonderful location and the authentic ambience of a Welsh Castle, Craig-y-Nos has plenty to offer. Whether you want a relaxing break, an over night stay, or if you are joining us as part of a function, you can be sure of a totally unique experience.

The Castle benefits from a number of bars and restaurants and is fully equipped to cater for conferences and wedding parties.

Craig-y-nos Castle has a wide variety of accommodation ranging from budget rooms to en-suite and luxury guest rooms overlooking the gardens. Each room is unique in design and is furnished in a traditional fashion in keeping with the Castle's history. The castle also benefits from Spa facilities, gymnasium and spa that enjoy unsurpassed panoramic views of the Brecon Beacons.

Craig-y-Nos Castle

Powys SA9 1GL
Email:
bookings_craigynos@hotmail.com
www.craigynoscastle.com

HOTEL FEATURES

- Fantastic Location
- Character Bedrooms
- Ghost Tours
- Beacons Spa Facilities
- Wonderful Public Rooms
- En suite Facilities

Haunted History

Old castles, with their colourful and often turbulent histories, often conjure up pictures of ghosts and paranormal goings-on. **Craig-y-Nos Castle** is no exception and has established a reputation amongst "ghost watchers" who have experienced apparitions, poltergeist activity and strange noises first hand. As the former home of Opera Diva Adelina Patti, who was embalmed in its cellars, and later as a Tuberculosis Hospital, where many succumbed to their illness, the Castle has a rich history of both dramatic and tragic events...

As well as being haunted by the Opera Diva herself, the Castle is home to many more spirits including a small boy accompanied by a soldier, often seen at the bottom of the staircase. The Nicolini Bar, formerly the Library of Patti's second husband Ernesto Nicolini, is haunted by a male spirit who is often heard shouting orders. There is also a well documented malevolent spirit who resides in the cellar.

A number of television programmes have been produced illustrating the paranormal activities at Craig-y-Nos Castle and due to the overwhelming interest from the general public wanting to experience them for themselves the castle now organises "Ghost Watch Tours".

The **Skirrid** Mountain Inn is situated in Llanvihangel Crucorney; a small village just off the A465; approximately 5 miles north from the centre of Abergavenny and 18 miles from Hereford.

It is reputed to be the oldest Inn in Wales and it's history can be traced back as far as the Norman Conquest.

The inn has an ancient wood-panelled restaurant where you can sit and enjoy delicious home cooked food from the menu. There are fireplaces with real fires, two bars, one with a pool table, an old ship's bell for calling last orders, and three comfortable luxury visitor's bedrooms, two with four poster beds.

The Skirrid Inn
Llanvihangel Crucorney,
Abergavenny,
Monmouthshire, NP7 8DH
Tel: 01873 890258
www.skirridmountaininn.co.uk/

Haunted History   **haunted**hotelguide.com

The **Skirrid Inn,** the oldest in Wales, is well known for its haunting happenings and there's good reason to take these "sightings" seriously due to the inn's gruesome history. The Skirrid has been an inn since 1110 but is most famous for its use as Judge Jeffrey's courtroom in the wake of the Monmouth rebellion. The brutal judge famously hanged 180 rebels in 1685 from a beam beneath the Skirrid's staircase. The beam stands today and bears chaffing marks from the hangman's rope.

No-one can be entirely sure who actually haunts the bedrooms and stairways of the Inn but many people believe that 'hanging' Judge Jeffreys could not rest, or that some of the 180 people he sent to the gallows have come back for revenge.

HOTEL FEATURES
- En suite facilities
- Four-poster beds
- Colour Television
- Tea and Coffee making
- Wonderful views

Stunning **Ross Castle**, situated on the shores of Lough Sheelin, dates back to 1536 and, not surprisingly, is steeped in history. The ghosts of two star-crossed lovers are often witnessed...

Situated amidst majestic trees in the tranquil countryside on the County Meath and Cavan border, Ross Castle commands magnificent views of Lough Sheelin, a 4500 acre lake famous for its brown trout and liberally stocked perch and large pike.

The secluded setting and spacious, comfortable accommodation offer the visitor an exclusive retreat. The Castle is the perfect place to relax and unwind, away from the stresses and strains of modern city life, or as a venue for a private party or function.

Ross Castle
Mountnugent
County Meath
Ireland
Tel: +353 (0) 43 81286
Email : book@ross-castle.com
www.ross-castle.com

Haunted History   **haunted**hotelguide.com

It all started back in 1536, when **Ross Castle** was first built. Legend has it that the Lord of Delvin, who built the castle, had a beautiful daughter, Sabina, who happened to fall in love with Orwin, the son of an Irish Lord. Fearing that their love would not be accepted by their families, they decided to elope. They set off in a sail boat but were unfortunately caught in a terrible storm. Orwin was tipped overboard and was killed instantly. Sabina was thrown out of the boat and was rescued by onlookers. They brought her back to the castle where she slept for three days. When she finally awoke, she found Orwin, who was laid out in the chapel on the grounds of Ross Castle. She died shortly after that.

HOTEL FEATURES
- Tea and Coffee making facilities.
- En suite Bedrooms
- Four-Poster Room
- Use of Leisure Facilities
  at Ross House

Kinnitty Castle

Kinnitty, Birr
County Offaly
Ireland
Tel: +353 (0)509 37318
Email: info@kinnittycastle.com
www.kinnittycastle.com

Stunning **Kinnitty Castle** has everything you would expect from an historic castle hotel and much more. We have our own resident ghost – The Monk!

Kinnitty Castle is located in the heart of Ireland, close to the picturesque village of Kinnitty in County Offaly. Approximately one hour 30 minutes from both Dublin and Shannon airports, it nestles in the foothills of the beautiful Slieve Bloom Mountains and is in Ireland's on designated Environment Park.

The whole area is steeped in Irish history and there is a wide range of things to see and do.

The hotel has 37 en suite bedrooms, all decorated in keeping with the castle's romantic old-world style. Wit two restaurants offering a selection of delicious dishes and two bars, the hotel is the ideal venue for holidays and special occasions alike. Our private panelled banqueting hall provides a secluded setting for weddings, conferences and themed functions.

Excellent cuisine, fine wines, open turf fires, candleligh and excellent service create a very warm and welcoming atmosphere that is special to Kinnitty Castle.

HOTEL FEATURES

- Luxury en suite accommodation
- Bars and Restaurants
- Gate Lodge Spa
- Activities such as shooting, fishing, tennis & equestrian sports

Haunted History

hauntedhotelguide.com

The Castle has a long and colourful history which dates back to ancient times. Located on an ancient druidic ceremonial ground, where leylines cross and mystical forces are prevalent, the area around Kinnitty is considered by many to be a very mystical and magical place. The castle is also known for its infamous ghostly guest… the monk.

The monk has often been seen wandering through the glorious Banqueting Hall, stunning both staff and visitors alike. He has been known to communicate with staff members on occasion, sometimes even prophesying about future events which have unbelievably come true! Other rooms throughout the castle are haunted, in particular the Geraldine Room and the Elizabeth room where eerie presences have been felt.

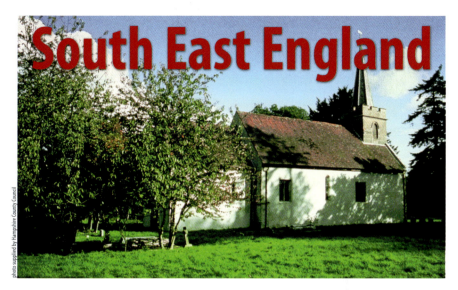

South East England

photo supplied by Hampshire County Council

WITH A POPULATION of over seven million, London is by far the largest city in Europe, sprawling over an area of 620 square miles. For first-time visitors a city sight-seeing tour by double-decker bus or by boat along the River Thames is a 'must'. Even for those already familiar with the main attractions, there's always something new in London. Buckingham Palace is now open to the public and proving a very popular attraction. Visitors are welcome from the end of July to the end of September and can visit the magnificent State Apartments as well as the Queen's Gallery, which is open all year, displaying many Royal treasures.

A visit to London is not complete without seeing the new Docklands – an 8½ square mile area with a fantastic range of old and new architecture (including Britain's tallest building), pubs and restaurants, shops, visitor attractions and parks – all just a short journey from the City Centre.

With its orchards, hopfields, bluebell woods and vineyards it's not surprising that Kent is known as 'The Garden of England'. Historic Kent towns like Canterbury, Rochester and Broadstairs are a contrast with Dover, still the busiest passenger seaport in Europe and gateway to the Channel Tunnel.

The South East has many and varied resorts, including Brighton, with its two piers, prom, graceful Georgian houses, antique shops, and the famous Royal Pavilion, built at the request of the Prince of Wales, later Prince Regent and George IV. Eastbourne is another fine family resort, while in the quieter nearby town of Bexhill, low tides reveal the remains of a forest – part of the land bridge by which Britain was joined to Europe 10,000 years ago.

Seaside towns also cluster along the Hampshire coast around the port of Southampton, itself a picturesque town. And in the extreme east of the county is Portsmouth, a town irrevocably tied to its seafaring heritage. There are naval museums and ships to see, including Nelson's famous flagship from Trafalgar, The Victory.

www.enjoyengland.com
www.visitlondon.com
www.visitsoutheastengland.com

South East England
Great Days Out: Visits and Attractions

BA London Eye
London • 0870 5000 600 www.londoneye.com
The world's highest observation wheel offers unrivalled views over London and beyond on its 30-minute slow-moving flight.

London Zoo• Gorilla Kingdom
London • 020 7722 3333
www.zsl.org
A brand new enclosure which is home to a colony of Western Lowland gorillas and colobus monkeys. Explore the forest pathways and then see these magnificent creatures in a natural clearing, surrounded by water.

The Living Rainforest
Near Newbury, Berkshire • 01635 202444
www.livingrainforest.org
Experience the sights, sounds and smells of a rainforest under glass. Gift shop, cafe.

Waddesdon Manor (NT)
Near Aylesbury, Bucks • 01296 653226
www.waddesdon.org.uk
A French Renaissance-style chateau housing the Rothschild Collection of art treasures. Superb gardens, aviary, restaurants, gift shops.

Bluereef Aquarium
Portsmouth, Hants • 023 9287 5222
www.bluereefaquarium.co.uk
The ultimate undersea safari. See the spectacular coral reef housed within a giant ocean display with its amazing walk-through tunnel.

Hollycombe Steam Collection
Liphook, Hants • 01428 724900
www.hollycombe.co.uk
Unique collection of working steam-powered attractions, including Edwardian fairground.

Dickens World
Chatham, Kent • 08702 411415
www.dickensworld.co.uk
A fascinating journey through the life and works of the famous author. Experience the sights, sounds and smells of the 19th century.

Eagle Heights
Eynsford, Kent • 01322 866577
www.eagleheights.co.uk
One of the UK's largest bird of prey centres with over 50 species of raptors. Daily flying demonstrations, and collection of reptiles and mammals.

Brooklands Museum
Weybridge, Surrey • 01932 857381
www.brooklandsmuseum.com
A history of aviation and motoring over the last 100 years, based at the original motor racing circuit. Try the Concorde Experience for yourself.

Ashdown Forest Llama Park
Near Forest Row, East Sussex • 01825 712040
www.llamapark.co.uk
A working farm where visitors can see breeding herds of llamas and alpacas. 'Walking with Llamas' - booking essential; large gift shop.

Weald & Downland Open Air Museum
Chichester, West Sussex • 01243 811363
www.wealddown.co.uk
Over 40 historic buildings carefully re-constructed, including medieval farmstead, working flour mill, and Victorian rural school.

Seaview Wildlife Encounter
Seaview, Isle of Wight • 01983 612261
www.flamingoparkiw.com
A world of wildlife awaits you at this award-winning park with its hand-on programme of events that has something for everyone - excitement, adventure, entertainment and education.

Local tourist offices offer free advice and guidance on all aspects of your holiday, from mapping out a touring route, local travel and excursions, to ideas on what to do and places to visit throughout the year. Don't hesitate to ask. . . !

South West England

photo supplied by Tourism Service, Plymouth City Council

WHATEVER SORT of holiday destination you're looking for, you'll find it in South-West England. As well as the elegant shops and Georgian crescents of Bath, other south-west towns have the very latest in big shopping centres, speciality shops and nightlife. There are stretches of wild moorland, chalk hills, limestone gorges and thatched-house villages and there are miles of golden sand washed by Atlantic breakers. From Orcombe Rocks, Exmouth to Studland Bay in Dorset, the Jurassic Coast Natural World Heritage Site gives a unique insight into life in the past through the rocks exposed along the 95 miles of beautiful coastline.

Devon has both coast and countryside. Plymouth on the south coast has been a naval base of the greatest importance to the defence of the realm since the days of Sir Francis Drake. The city was hastily rebuilt after destruction in the Second World War, but nothing can spoil the glorious vista of the Sound viewed from Plymouth Hoe where Drake finished his game of bowls.

Cornwall reaches into the Atlantic Ocean for almost 100 miles. Take a walk along any part of this strikingly beautiful coast, enjoy a cream tea in one of the charming villages sheltering in a cove and you will understand why Cornwall has been the inspiration for so many artists, novelists and poets. Often free from frost in winter, the soft spring climate favours Cornwall as an ideal destination for holiday breaks.

Say Somerset and most people would automatically think of cider, Cheddar cheese and county cricket matches. But there's a lot more to Somerset – there's Exmoor which is Lorna Doone territory and home to the wild Exmoor ponies and herds of red deer. The National Park of Exmoor has a coastline with some marvellous clifftop walks. Further along this coast are Somerset's main seaside resorts, Minehead and Burnham-on-Sea.

www.westcountrynow.com

South West England
Great Days Out: Visits and Attractions

Flambards
Helston, Cornwall • 01326 573404
www.flambards.co.uk
More than just a theme park, with thrill rides, Flambards Victorian Village, Britain in the Blitz, aviation display, award-winning gardens; restaurants and cafes.

The Eden Project
Near St Austell, Cornwall • 01726 811911
www.edenproject.com
A gateway into the fascinating interaction of plants and people. Two gigantic geodesic conservatories - the Humid Tropics Biome and the Warm Temperate Biome - set amidst landscaped outdoor terraces.

Quince Honey Farm
South Molton, Devon • 01769 572401
www.quincehoney.co.uk
The world's largest living honey bee exhibition, where the hives can be viewed in complete safety. Ideal for all ages, with fascinating videos and well-stocked shop.

Escot Historic Gardens, Maze and Fantasy Woodlands
Ottery St Mary, Devon • 01404 822188
www.escot-devon.co.uk
For people who love Nature - paths, trails, vistas, beautiful flowers, shrubs and specimen trees. Play areas, pets' corner, restaurant - and lots more!

World of Country Life
Exmouth, Devon • 01395 274533
www.worldofcountrylife.co.uk
Take a walk down memory lane - re-created streets and exhibitions of vintage transport and agricultural machinery. Children's play area and pets centre.

The Jurassic Coast
East Devon + Dorset
www.jurassiccoast.com
England's first natural World Heritage Site - 95 miles of unspoilt cliffs and beaches, tracing over 185 million years of Earth's history.

Abbotsbury Swannery
Near Weymouth, Dorset • 01305 871858
www.abbotsbury-tourism.co.uk
Up to 1000 free-flying swans – help feed them twice daily. Baby swans hatch May/June. AV show, coffee shop and gift shop.

Haynes Motor Museum
Near Yeovil, Somerset • 01963 440804
www.haynesmotormuseum.co.uk
Magnificent collection of over 250 vintage, veteran and classic cars, and 50 motorcycles.

Jane Austen Centre
Bath • 01225 443000
www.janeausten.co.uk
Explore the Bath of one of the historic city's most famous residents, and its place in her work. Exhibition of Regency clothes, shop with selection of related books, stationery and crafts.

Dunster Water Mill
Dunster, Somerset • 01643 821759
The West Country's finest working water mill, set alongside the River Avill. See how flour is produced, then visit the Mill Shop where stoneground floor, home-made muesli and other products are available.

Wookey Hole Caves
Near Wells, Somerset • 01749 672243
www.wookey.co.uk
Britain's most spectacular underground caverns, with new attractions and great new facilities. Try making your own paper using original Victorian machinery.

Cholderton Rare Breeds Farm Park
Near Salisbury, Wiltshire • 01980 629438
www.choldertoncharliesfarm.com
Rare and endangered breeds of British farm animals, plus Rabbit World with over 50 varieties. Pig racing (Pork Stakes) in peak season.

East of England

photo by Andy Tryner © North East Lincolnshire Council

EAST ANGLIA, once a Saxon kingdom cut off from the rest of England by marshland and forest, remains to this day a relatively unexplored part of Britain. It is an area of low, chalky hills, pleasant market towns, working windmills adding charm to the fields, wide sweeping views over the flattest land and glorious sunsets. Along East Anglia's North Sea coast, the visitor can choose between bustling seaside resorts or long stretches of deserted sandy beaches. Boating enthusiasts come from all over the world for holidays afloat on the Norfolk Broads, an ancient man-made network of shallow tree-fringed lakes, rivers and canals. East Anglia's inland towns are full of history and proud to tell their stories at visitor centres and museums. Specialist museums abound. The Imperial War Museum at Duxford Airfield has the largest collection of military and civil aircraft in Britain. Duxford was a Battle of Britain station and the flatness of East Anglia gave it the wartime distinction of having the largest number of airfields in the country. Steam, vintage and miniature railway museums, classic car collections, bicycle museums: East Anglia has them all, as well as the famous Lace Museum (with magnifying glasses provided) in Norfolk, a Working Silk Museum at the restored silk mills in Braintree, and a Motorboat Museum in Basildon tracing the history of motor boats, racing hydroplanes and leisure boats. At Lowestoft harbour you can step aboard the last survivor of more than 3000 drifters that came every autumn to Yarmouth and Lowestoft, following the plentiful shoals of herring. Visual displays portray the hardships of the herring workers, male and female, who brought prosperity to the two ports for more than a century but only poverty to themselves. It was a different way of life – above stairs at least – for the inhabitants of the great mansion houses of East Anglia in their heyday. The Queen's favourite country seat in England, Sandringham House, is open to the public from the end of July to the end of October.

www.visiteastofengland.com

East of England
Great Days Out: Visits and Attractions

Whipsnade Wild Animal Park
Dunstable, Bedfordshire • 01582 872171
www.zsl.org/whipsnade
See rare and endangered species from around the world. Visitors can take a trip through the Woodland Bird Walk and visit the children's farm in 600 acres of parkland.

Linton Zoo
Linton, Cambs • 01223 891308
www.lintonzoo.co.uk
The emphasis is on conservation and education. with lots of rare and exotic animals. Set in 16 acres of beautiful gardens, with picnic and children's play areas.

Colchester Zoo
Colchester, Essex • 01206 331292
www.colchester-zoo.co.uk
Set in 60 acres of grounds, over 150 species in award-winning enclosures. Over 15 daily displays from elephant bathtime to penguin parades.

Colne Valley Railway
Castle Hedingham • 01787 461174
www.colnevalleyrailway.co.uk
Take a ride on an award-winning country railway. Visitor Centre and new Garden Railway; regular 'Days Out with Thomas the Tank Engine'.

Knebworth House
Near Stevenage, Herts • 01438 812661
www.knebworthhouse.com
Home of the Lytton family since 1490, with fine collections of manuscripts, portraits and furniture. Set in 250 acre country park with formal gardens and large adventure playground. Gift shop, cafe.

Hatfield House
Hatfield, Herts • 01707 287010
www.hatfield-house.co.uk
Jacobean house built by the Cecil family. Rich in paintings, furniture, tapestries and armour. Extensive gardens, recently restored.

National Fishing Heritage Centre
Grimsby, N.E. Lincs • 01472 323345
www.nelincs.gov.uk
Tells the story of fishermen, their boats, and the waters they fished in. The dangers and hardships of life at sea are vividly re-created.

Sandringham
Near King's Lynn, Norfolk • 01553 612908
www.sandringham-estate.co.uk
The Queen's country estate – 600 acres of gardens and lakes; house and museum of royal vehicles also open to public.

Pettitts Animal Adventure Park
Near Great Yarmouth • 01493 700094
www.pettittsadventurepark.co.uk
Three parks in one - fun for all the family. Rides, play area, adventure golf course, animals galore.

Merrivale Model Village
Great Yarmouth • 01493 842097
www.greatyarmouthmodelvillage.co.uk
Model village set in an acre of landscaped gardens - watch out for the bank robber and the streaker! New Merrival Castle. Tea room and shop.

Dinosaur Adventure Park
Weston Park, Norwich • 01603 876310
www.dinosaurpark.co.uk
Follow the Dinosaur Trail and meet giants from the past. Make friends with animals, from hedgehogs to wallabies, bugs and snakes, in the secret animal garden.

National Horse Racing Museum
Newmarket, Suffolk • 01638 667333
www.nhrm.co.uk
Five permanent galleries tell the story of the development of the "sport of kings" over 400 years. Special exhibition for 2007. Meet retired jockeys and ride the horse simulator.

Kentwell Hall & Gardens
Long Melford, Suffolk • 01787 310207
www.kentwell.co.uk
A lovely Elizabethan house, brought back to life as a unique family home. Award-winning re-creations of everyday life in Tudor and WWII times. Gardens, rare breeds farm, maze, plus lots more.

> Local tourist offices offer free advice and guidance on all aspects of your holiday, from mapping out a touring route, local travel and excursions, to ideas on what to do and places to visit throughout the year. Don't hesitate to ask...!

The Midlands

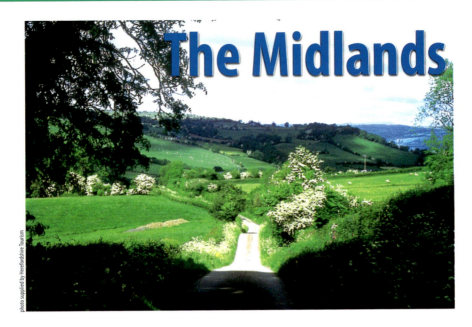

photo supplied by Herefordshire Tourism

FOLLOWING The Romantic Road is not what immediately comes to mind when the English Midlands are being considered as a holiday destination. Nevertheless, the Romantic Road is a very suitable title for a guide to the picture-postcard villages of the Cotswolds which is available from Cheltenham Tourism. The gentle hills and honey-coloured houses of the Cotswolds are deservedly popular with tourists in summer. Quieter, but just as beautiful in their way, are other scenic areas of the Midlands: the Wye Valley, the Vale of Evesham, Sherwood Forest, once the haunt of the legendary Robin Hood and, near the Welsh border, the wooded valleys known as the Marches around the towns of Hereford and Shrewsbury

In a secluded valley in this area a discovery was made that changed the face of the world when Abraham Darby perfected his revolutionary techniques for the mass production of cast iron. Today there are no fewer than seven museums in the Gorge, which has been designated a World Heritage Site.

To keep the children happy there is also a Teddy Bear Museum and the Ironbridge Toy Museum. Children are welcome at the Heritage Motor Centre at Gaydon, the largest collection of British cars in the world; quad biking over rough terrain track is available for children.

Staffordshire is the home of the Potteries and some of the best china and porcelain in the world is made there. Visit Stoke-on-Trent for the complete China Experience, factory tours, ceramic museums and, to take home as a souvenir of the Midlands, world famous names like Wedgwood, Royal Doulton and Spode china at amazing discounts.

www.visitheartofengland.com
www.enjoyenglandseastmidlands.com

The Midlands
Great Days Out: Visits and Attractions

Donington Grand Prix Collection
Castle Donington • 01332 811027
www.doningtoncollection.com
The world's largest collection of Grand Prix racing cars in five halls of fame. The largest collection of Mclarens under one roof.

Conkers – National Forest Centre
Moira, Leicestershire • 01283 216633
www.visitconkers.com
Award-winning attraction at the heart of the National Forest. Explore the woodland trails, relax by the lakeside. Woodland garden, adventure playground, restaurant and shop.

National Space Centre
Leicester, Leics • 0116 261 0261
www.spacecentre.co.uk
The UK's largest attraction dedicated to space science and astronomy. The stories, personalities and technology of the past and present are used to explain how it will affect our future.

Natural World Centre
Near Lincoln • 01522 688868
www.naturalworldcentre.com
Our Changing World exhibition, eco-friendly shopping, walks through wildlife haven. Lots of special events, workshops, children's activities.

Acton Scott Historic Working Farm
Church Stretton • 01694 781306
www.shropshire.gov.uk/museums
Practical demonstrations of traditional country skills with visits from the farrier, wheelwright and blacksmith. Waymarked walks, friendly animals, shop with country crafts, cafe.

Ceramica
Burslem, Staffs • 01782 832001
www.ceramicauk.com
Ceramica is a unique experience and a great day out for the whole family. Follow the path from clay right through to a finished product.

Blackbrook Zoological Park
Winkhill, Staffs • 01538 308293
www.blackbrookzoologicalpark.co.uk
Many unusual species of birds, including storks and cranes. Children's farm, pets' area, insect and reptile house. Open all year except Christmas/ New Year.

Heritage Motor Centre
Gaydon, Warwickshire • 01926 641188
www.heritage-motor-centre.co.uk
The largest collection of British cars in the world. 4-wheel drive demonstration circuit, children's roadway, cafe and gift shop.

Stratford-upon-Avon Butterfly Farm
Stratford-upon-Avon • 01789 299288
www.butterflyfarm.co.uk
Hundreds of free-flying exotic butterflies in a natural jungle setting. Visit Insect City with leaf-cutting ants, giant millipedes and lots more - all safely behind glass!

Coventry Transport Museum
Coventry, West Midlands • 024 7623 4270
www.transport-museum.com
The largest display in the world of British-made road transport, from buses to bikes. Tiatsa Model Collection, Coventry Blitz Experience and lots more.

Thinktank at Millennium Point
Birmingham • 0121 202 2222
www.thinktank.ac
10 themed galleries help us understand how science and technology shape our lives. You can examine the past, investigate the present and explore what the future may bring.

Avoncroft Museum
Near Bromsgrove, Worcs • 01527 831363
www.avoncroft.org.uk
Historic buildings saved from destruction, including a working windmill, furnished houses and the National Telephone Kiosk Collection.

The North of England

photo supplied by Scarborough Borough Council

THERE ARE SOME PEOPLE who prefer a holiday where every day is packed with action and every evening filled with fun. Others see a holiday as the exact opposite, a chance to get some peace and quiet in the wide open spaces. Whatever sort of holidaymaker you are, the North of England has plenty to offer you. The North has some of the best living museums and 'hands-on' visitor centres in Britain, where the latest presentation techniques are equally fascinating to adults and children. How does the world look to a fish, a dog, a bee? Find out – and learn to make rainbows too – at the Colour Museum in the once-grimy city of Bradford. Also in Bradford is the National Media Museum which has Britain's biggest cinema screen, a thousand times bigger than your TV screen at home – and not content with that, it also has the world's only Cinerama cinema, the world's biggest lens, smallest camera and first-ever photographic likeness! Just as interesting are the smaller heritage museums to be found in practically every town and village in the North. Britain's National Railway Museum is in York, the birthplace of the steam railway. If a day trip behind a steam engine is more your style, ask for the Yorkshire Tourist Board's leaflet 'Steaming Along' with details of seven steam railways and the dates of the kiddies' specials – the Thomas the Tank Engine week-ends.

The seaside resorts of the North have provided happiness for children and relaxation for Mums and Dads for generations. In Lancashire, on the west coast, Southport, St Annes, Blackpool, Morecambe – often it's the same resort families choose year after satisfied year. The twin resorts of Whitley Bay and Tynemouth are on the North Tyneside coast. From bright lights to walking on the fells, from heritage visits to Sunday shopping, you'll find them all in the North of England!

www.golakes.co.uk
www.visitnortheastengland.com
www.visitenglandsnorthwest.com
www.yorkshire.com

North of England Great Days Out: Visits and Attractions

Hat Works
Stockport, Cheshire • 0845 8330975
www.hatworks.org.uk
In a restored Grade II Listed Victorian mill, the UK's only museum dedicated to hats and headwear. Demonstrations of working machinery, AV shows, and an extensive collection of hats. Family Fun area, guided tours.

Trotters World of Animals
Bassenthwaite, Cumbria • 017687 76239
www.trottersworld.com
Award-winning wildlife park set amidst picturesque Lakeland fells, with a full programme of activities throughout the year. Indoor and outdoor play areas; picnic area.

Cumberland Pencil Museum
Keswick, Cumbria • 017687 73626
www.pencilmuseum.co.uk
The fascinating history of the humble pencil, from the discovery of Borrowdale graphite to present day manufacture. See the world's largest colouring pencil. Shop.

Killhope Lead Mining Museum
Near Cowshill, Co Durham • 01388 537505
www.durham.gov.uk/killhope
Get a glimpse of a vanished way of life with a trip to Park Level Mine, and a re-creation of the appalling working and living conditions of the late 19th century. A real 'hands on' adventure which brings the past vividly to life.

National Football Museum
Preston, Lancashire• 01772 908442
www.nationalfootballmuseum.com
The story of the world's greatest game. In two distinctive halves, it can be enjoyed by supporters of all ages. Shop and restaurant.

The Lowry
Salford Quays, Manchester • 0870 787 5788
www.thelowry.com
A landmark building of stainless steel and glass houses galleries and exhibitions, theatres, workshops and activities, restaurants and bars.

Knowsley Safari Park
Prescot • 0151 430 9009
www.knowsley.com/safari
Around 30 species of mammal roaming 200 hectares of land. Also Children's Lake Farm, the Bug House, sealion shows, miniature railway, amusement park rides and bird of prey displays.

Alnwick Castle
Alnwick, Northumberland • 01665 511100
www.alnwickcastle.com
Famous as Hogwarts School in the Harry Potter films. Visit the Knights School and Alnwick Garden, with its huge Treehouse and Poison Garden.

Centre for Life
Newcastle, Tyne & Wear • 0191-243 8210
www.lifesciencecentre.org.uk
The secret of life – how it works, what it means. A thrilling motion-simulator ride, live theatre, 3D interactive exhibits, virtual reality – an unforgettable experience.

Eden Camp Modern History Museum
Malton, North Yorkshire • 01653 697777
www.edencamp.co.uk
This award-winning museum will take you back to wartime Britain where you can experience the sights, sounds and smells of World War II.

Magna Science Adventure Centre
Hull, South Yorkshire • 01709 720002
www.visitmagna.co.uk
The UK's first Science Adventure Centre explores the four elements of Fire, Earth, Air and Water. Experience sound and light shows, fire giant water cannons, and lots more!

The Deep
Hull, South Yorkshire • 01482 381000
www.thedeep.co.uk
A journey from the beginning of time telling the story of the oceans, using a combination of hands-on activities, AV presentations and living exhibits.

symbols

 Totally non-smoking

 Children Welcome

 Suitable for Disabled Guests

🐕 Pets Welcome

🌲 Christmas Breaks

🍷 Licensed

London
(Central & Greater)

 # The Athena

110-114 SUSSEX GARDENS, HYDE PARK, LONDON W2 1UA
Tel: 0207 706 3866; Fax: 0207 262 6143
E-Mail: athena@stavrouhotels.co.uk www.stavrouhotels.co.uk

TREAT YOURSELVES TO A QUALITY HOTEL AT AFFORDABLE PRICES

The Athena is a newly completed family run hotel in a restored Victorian building. Professionally designed, including a lift to all floors and exquisitely decorated, we offer our clientele the ambience and warm hospitality necessary for a relaxing and enjoyable stay. Ideally located in a beautiful tree-lined avenue, extremely well-positioned for sightseeing London's famous sights and shops; Hyde Park, Madame Tussaud's, Oxford Street, Marble Arch, Knightsbridge, Buckingham Palace and many more are all within walking distance.

Travel connections to all over London are excellent, with Paddington and Lancaster Gate Stations, Heathrow Express, A2 Airbus and buses minutes away.
Our tastefully decorated bedrooms have en suite bath/shower rooms, satellite colour TV, bedside telephones, tea/coffee making facilities. Hairdryers, trouser press, laundry and ironing facilities available on request. Ample car parking.

Stavrou Hotels is a family-run group of hotels.
We offer quality and convenience at affordable rates.
A VERY WARM WELCOME AWAITS YOU.

Single Rooms from £50-£65
Double/Twin Rooms from £64-£95
Triple & Family Rooms from £28 per person
All prices include full English breakfast plus VAT.

Our hotels accept all major Credit cards, but some charges may apply.

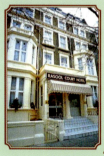

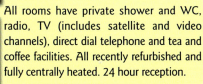

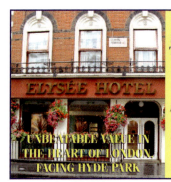
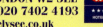

 # Queens Hotel

33 Anson Road, Tufnell Park, LONDON N7

Tel: 0207 607 4725; Fax: 0207 697 9725

E-Mail: queens@stavrouhotels.co.uk   www.stavrouhotels.co.uk

The Queens Hotel is a large double-fronted Victorian building standing in its own grounds five minutes' walk from Tufnell Park Station.
Quietly situated with ample car parking spaces; 15 minutes to West End and close to London Zoo, Hampstead and Highgate. Two miles from King's Cross and St Pancras Stations. Many rooms en suite.

All prices include full English Breakfast plus VAT.
Children half-price. Discounts on longer stays

Stavrou Hotels is a family-run group of hotels.
We offer quality and convenience at affordable rates.
A VERY WARM WELCOME AWAITS YOU.

Single Rooms from £25-£34
Double/Twin Rooms from £40-£54
Triple & Family Rooms from £18 per person

Our hotels accept all major
Credit cards, but some
charges may apply.

Cornwall

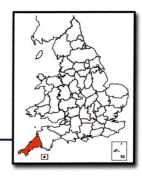

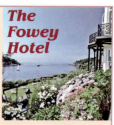

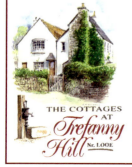

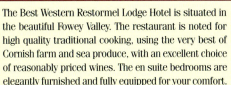

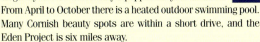

10 Things you didn't Know about Cornwall

• Using the South West Coast Path you can walk around the entire 400 km coast of Cornwall! The South West Coast Path is one of the UK's most spectacular walking routes and with over 4000 km of inland paths, Cornwall is a hikers' delight.

• Warmed by the Gulf Stream, Cornwall has a unique climate and many sub-tropical plant species thrive here. There are over 70 gardens open to the public, from large formal estate gardens such as Lanhydrock to rescued and restored treasures such as the Lost Gardens of Heligan.

• One of the UK's most visited attractions is located in Cornwall. The Eden Project attracts 1.5 million visitors each year and it provides an entertaining and educational insight into man's relationship with plants.

• Cornwall's heritage is rich in myth, folklore and legend. From strange Bronze Age stone monuments to King Arthur's famous castle at Tintagel. Cornwall's industrial heritage is also hugely important, so much so that a bid has been made to UNESCO for World Heritage Site status to help preserve these landscapes.

• Marazion near Penzance is the oldest town in Cornwall and it dates back to 1257. It is a popular destination for those visiting the mysterious island of St Michael's Mount. At low tide visitors can walk across to the mount from Marazion by means of a causeway.

• The first sighting of the approaching Spanish Armada was from Cornwall on July 19th 1588. Watchers on Halzephron Cliff watched the Armada as it approached Mounts Bay. Rumour has it that rather than fight they ran and hid...

• Cornwall boasts some of Europe's finest surfing beaches and each year Newquay hosts a number of international surfing competitions. But if surfing isn't enough to get the adrenaline going, the growing sport of kite surfing is guaranteed to!

• You don't need to head to London for fine dining! With an increasing number of top national chefs beating a path to the county, visitors are spoilt for choice. Great pubs, stylish restaurants and beachside cafes all serving a fantastic choice of local cuisine.

• Cornwall has beaches to rival the Costa del Sol! The Porthminster Beach St Ives was recently voted the 3rd best beach in the world because of its great location, golden sands, Blue Flag status and great choice of bars/cafes.

• Outside London, Cornwall has the largest concentration of artists in the UK. It even has its very own Tate Gallery which occupies a spectacular position overlooking Porthmeor Beach in St Ives.

Near Perranporth

Welcome to Greenmeadow Holiday Cottages

Greenmeadow Holiday Cottages are a group of six cottages, situated in a rural setting, yet only 400 yards from the local shop and 500 yards to the pub which serves excellent food and real ale.

The holiday cottages are three miles from Perranporth's golden sands on the north coast of Cornwall.

All sleep up to six people, two cottages welcome pets and all are non-smoking. Three cottages have one en suite bedroom on the ground floor.

• **New for 2007
Children's Adventure Play Area.**

• **There is also a shared BBQ area**

We are open all year and offer short break holiday cottage accommodation out of season.

Greenmeadow Cottages, Bridge Road, Goonhavern, Truro, Cornwall TR4 9NN • 01872 540 483
e-mail: info@greenmeadow-cottages.co.uk
www.greenmeadow-cottages.co.uk

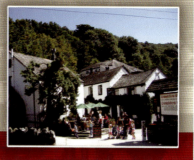

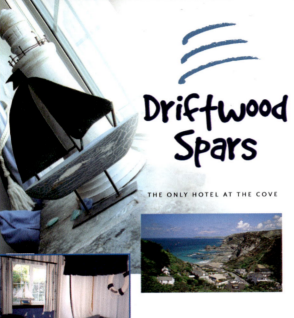

Other specialised holiday guides from FHG

Recommended **INNS & PUBS** OF BRITAIN

Recommended **COUNTRY HOTELS** OF BRITAIN

The bestselling and original **PETS WELCOME!**

The GOLF GUIDE, *Where to Play, Where to Stay* IN BRITAIN & IRELAND

COAST & COUNTRY HOLIDAYS

SELF-CATERING HOLIDAYS IN BRITAIN

BED & BREAKFAST STOPS

CARAVAN & CAMPING HOLIDAYS

CHILDREN WELCOME! Family Holiday & Days Out Guide

BRITAIN'S BEST LEISURE & RELAXATION GUIDE

Published annually: available in all good bookshops or direct from the publisher:
FHG Guides, Abbey Mill Business Centre, Seedhill, Paisley PA1 1TJ
Tel: 0141 887 0428 • Fax: 0141 889 7204
E-mail: admin@fhguides.co.uk • Web: www.holidayguides.com

Dalswinton

A Victorian stone-built house standing in 10 acres of gardens and meadowland in the glorious Vale of Lanherne, midway between Padstow and Newquay. Overlooking the village of St Mawgan, with views to the sea at Mawgan Porth, Dalswinton offers a warm welcome, friendly atmosphere, and great food prepared with fresh local produce.

We are totally non-smoking, and are not suitable for children under 16.

- Dogs free of charge and allowed everywhere except the restaurant
- 8 acres of private meadowland for dog exercise
- Dog-friendly beach 1.5 miles
- Bed & Breakfast from £39.00 per person per night
- Weekly rates available. Special offers Oct/Mar/Apr.
- Heated outdoor pool (in season). Car parking
- All rooms en suite, with tea/coffee making facilities, colour TV and radio
- Residents' bar, and restaurant serving breakfast and 3-course dinner
- Self-catering Garden Lodge (sleeps 3 adults)
- Easy access to Newquay Airport, Padstow and the Eden Project

Proprietors: Stuart and Sal Hope
Dalswinton House, St Mawgan-in-Pydar, Cornwall TR8 4EZ
Tel: 01637 860385
Visit us at www.dalswinton.com   e-mail: dalswintonhouse@tiscali.co.uk

Devon

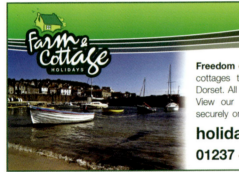

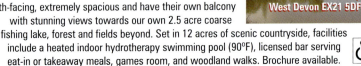

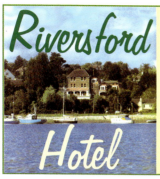

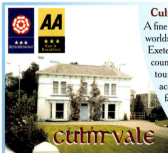

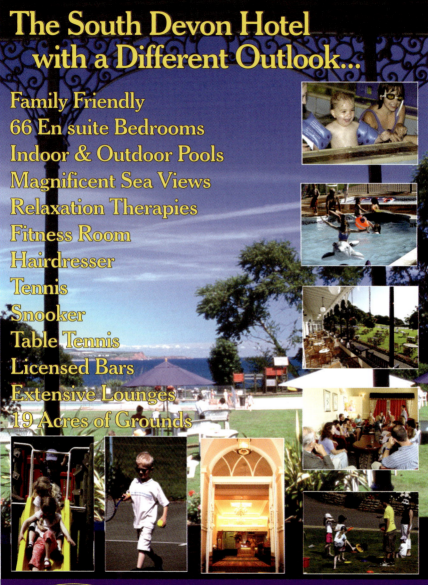

White Hart
Hotel • Exeter

One of Exeter's most historic inns, the White Hart Hotel retains much of its heritage and charm and yet offers the business or leisure visitor all the facilities and amenities of modern living.

The White Hart boasts 55 en suite rooms. Located in a central position within the old city walls, it's ideally situated to enjoy all the city has to offer, from its famous Gothic Cathedral to the newly opened shopping centre.

The White Hart offers meeting and function rooms with a choice of eating areas, a walled secret garden, an extensive selection of freshly cooked meals, fine cask ales and a comprehensive wine list – all tastes are catered for.

White Hart Hotel
66 South Street, Exeter EX1 1EE
Tel: 01392 279897 • Fax: 01392 250159
E-mail: whitehart.exeter@marstons.co.uk

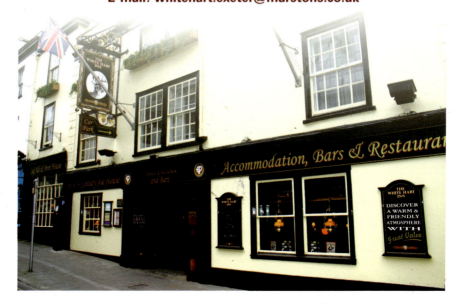

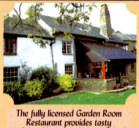

symbols

Totally non-smoking		Pets Welcome	
Children Welcome		Christmas Breaks	
Suitable for Disabled Guests		Licensed	

symbols

🚭	Totally non-smoking		🐕	Pets Welcome
🐎	Children Welcome		⊛	Christmas Breaks
♿	Suitable for Disabled Guests		⚱	Licensed

Dorset

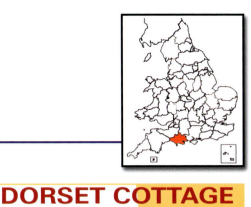

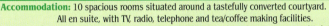

CALIFORNIA BARN Swanage BH19 2RS
Tel: 01929 425049 • Fax: 01929 421695
e-mail: delahays@hotmail.com • www.californiacottage.co.uk

A 200-year-old stone barn set in 11 acres of lush meadows with stunning sea views. The beautiful Jurassic Coast, recently designated a World Heritage Site, and the South West Coast Path lie only two fields away. Swanage, with all its family facilities is only one mile away. Converted and furnished to a high standard, the three bedrooms and three bathrooms can accommodate up to 10. The location of one bedroom and one bathroom on the ground floor make it ideal for wheelchair users and those with limited mobility. Visitors also have access to a large studio/meeting room. Arts tuition, wildlife and archaeological talks/tours can be arranged. No smoking. Pets allowed; livery available.

Short breaks available September to June (excl. Christmas and New Year).
£275-£575 for 3/4 nights • £475-£1000 per week

This comfortably furnished bungalow, with attractive garden in a quiet cul-de-sac at West Bay, overlooks open field, only three minutes' walk to the harbour and beach. Ideal for family holidays, walking, fishing, visiting many places of interest or just relaxing.

Three bedrooms, two double and one twin bedded, sleeping six • Sitting room with colour TV • Well equipped kitchen/dining room. • Bathroom and separate toilet • Garden and parking space • Open all year • Out of season short breaks available • Personally supervised • Details from:

Robins
Meadway, West Bay, Bridport

Mrs B. Loosmore, Barlands, Lower Street, West Chinnock, Crewkerne, Somerset TA18 7PT Tel: 01935 881790

Peace and Tranquillity

Small select park with stunning views over Jurassic Coastline

GORSELANDS CARAVAN PARK
West Bexington-on-Sea · Dorset

• **Excellent beach fishing**
• **Pets Welcome • Caravans & Apartments**
• **Camping nearby mid July-August • Shop and Launderette**
• **Village Pub 100 yards • Beach and car park one mile**

Tel: 01308 897232 • Fax: 01308 897239
www.gorselands.co.uk
e-mail: info@gorselands.co.uk
West Bexington-on Sea,
Near Bridport, Dorset DT2 9DJ

BH&HPA
BRITISH HOLIDAY & HOME PARKS ASSOCIATION
SILVER

English Tourism Council
★★★★
HOLIDAY PARK

A useful index of towns/counties appears at the back of this book

Looking for holiday accommodation?
for details of hundreds of properties
throughout the UK including
comprehensive coverage of all areas of Scotland try:

www.holidayguides.com

Gloucestershire

THE FOUNTAIN
INN & LODGE

Parkend, Royal Forest of Dean, Gloucestershire GL15 4JD.

Traditional village inn, well known locally for its excellent meals and real ales. A Forest Fayre menu offers such delicious main courses as Lamb Steak In Woodland Berry Sauce and Gloucester Sausage in Onion Gravy, together with a large selection of curries, vegetarian dishes, and other daily specials.

Centrally situated in one of England's foremost wooded areas, the inn makes an ideal base for sightseeing, or for exploring some of the many peaceful forest walks nearby.

All bedrooms (including one specially adapted for the less able) are en suite, decorated and furnished to an excellent standard, and have television and tea/coffee making facilities. Various half-board breaks are available throughout the year.

Tel: 01594 562189 • Fax: 01594 564438 • e-mail: thefountaininn@aol.com • www.thefountaininnandlodge.com

THE *Old Stocks Hotel*
The Square, Stow-on-the-Wold GL54 1AF
Tel: 01451 830666 • Fax: 01451 870014
e-mail: fhg@oldstockshotel.co.uk

Ideal base for touring this beautiful area. Tasteful guest rooms in keeping with the hotel's old world character, yet with modern amenities. Mouth-watering menus offering a wide range of choices. Special bargain breaks also available. 3-terraced patio garden.   *HETB/AA* ★★

www.oldstockshotel.co.uk

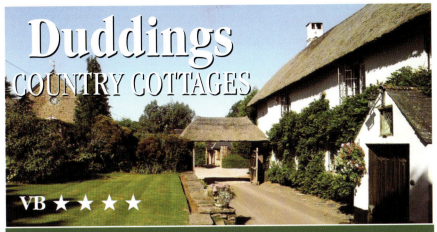

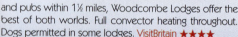

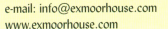

Wiltshire

Berkshire

symbols

	Totally non-smoking		Pets Welcome
	Children Welcome		Christmas Breaks
	Suitable for Disabled Guests		Licensed

Buckinghamshire

Hampshire

Ponies in the New Forest. photo: Joe Low

Visit the FHG website
www.holidayguides.com
for details of the wide choice of accommodation
featured in the full range of FHG titles

Isle of Wight

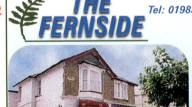

Kent

symbols

 Totally non-smoking

 Children Welcome

 Suitable for Disabled Guests

 Pets Welcome

 Christmas Breaks

 Licensed

Oxfordshire

The Springs is an attractive Tudor-style country house located in the heart of the Thames Valley. Set in landscaped gardens, overlooking a spring-fed lake from which the hotel takes its name, we retain those traditional values associated with the great Country Houses of England.

Leisure facilities include an outdoor swimming pool, sauna, croquet lawn, putting green, coarse fishing on the Thames and an 18 hole par 72 golf course.

Golf Breaks from as little as £160.00 (2 nights, 3 rounds)

Your stay here would not be complete without trying the gourmet skills of our award winning Chefs, in the AA Rosette Lakeside Restaurant or the Clubhouse, both of which have a well-deserved local reputation for excellence.

We are also licensed to host civil, naming and same sex ceremonies.

The Springs Hotel and Golf Club
Wallingford Road, North Stoke, Wallingford, Oxfordshire OX10 6BE
Tel: 01491 836687 • Fax: 01491 836877
e-mail: info@thespringshotel.com
www.thespringshotel.com

AA
★★★
HOTEL

Surrey

The Hurtwood Inn Hotel

Set at the heart of the picturesque village of Peaslake, in the beautiful Surrey Hills, this family-run privately owned hotel has an enviable reputation for the individuality and quality of its cuisine and hospitality

Ideally placed to explore some of England's finest countryside, such as Leith Tower Hill, South of England's highest point with breathtaking views, the National Trust properties of Polesden Lacey and Clandon Park, and nearby the historic county town of Guildford. 21 tastefully furnished en suite bedrooms. 'Oscars' Restaurant with superb local reputation, serving modern and traditional cuisine in the intimate dining room.

Hurtwood Inn Hotel, Walking Bottom, Peaslake, Near Guildford, Surrey GU5 9RR
Tel:.01306 730851 • Fax: 01306 731390

e-mail: sales@hurtwoodinnhotel.com • www.hurtwoodinnhotel.com

Hotel of the Year • Millenium South East England Tourist Board Award 2000 (under 50 bedrooms)

symbols

	Totally non-smoking			Pets Welcome
	Children Welcome			Christmas Breaks
	Suitable for Disabled Guests			Licensed

FREE or REDUCED RATE entry to Holiday Visits and Attractions – see our
READERS' OFFER VOUCHERS on pages 199-206

East Sussex

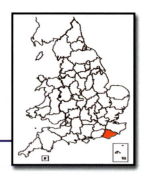

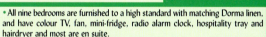

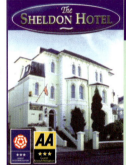

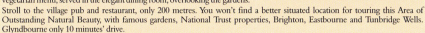
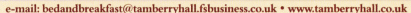

Other specialised holiday guides from **FHG**

Recommended **INNS & PUBS** OF BRITAIN

Recommended **COUNTRY HOTELS** OF BRITAIN

The bestselling and original **PETS WELCOME!**

The **GOLF GUIDE,** *Where to Play, Where to Stay* IN BRITAIN & IRELAND

COAST & COUNTRY HOLIDAYS

SELF-CATERING HOLIDAYS IN BRITAIN

BED & BREAKFAST STOPS

CARAVAN & CAMPING HOLIDAYS

CHILDREN WELCOME! Family Holiday & Days Out Guide

BRITAIN'S BEST LEISURE & RELAXATION GUIDE

Published annually: available in all good bookshops or direct from the publisher:
FHG Guides, Abbey Mill Business Centre, Seedhill, Paisley PA1 1TJ
Tel: 0141 887 0428 • Fax: 0141 889 7204
E-mail: admin@fhguides.co.uk • Web: www.holidayguides.com

West Sussex

The Woodstock House Hotel
Charlton, Near Chichester PO18 0HU

In the heart of the magnificent South Downs, just a few miles from Chichester and convenient for Goodwood, Woodstock House Hotel is converted from a former farmhouse. Bed & Breakfast is available in 13 en suite bedrooms, with all modern amenities, set round an attractive courtyard garden. One ground floor room is available in a separate annexe.

Tel/Fax: 01243 811666
info@woodstockhousehotel.co.uk
www.woodstockhousehotel.co.uk

Park House Hotel
4 St Georges Road, Worthing BN11 2DS

The Park House is owned and run as a Guest House by the Smith family who will greet you with genuine hospitality, instantly making you feel at home. The wealth of beautiful art and furniture add to the stylish atmosphere which runs throughout the tastefully furnished en suite bedrooms, all of which have Sky Sports and tea and coffee facilities. *The Hotel is located less than a minute's walk from Worthing's fishing beach, and a 10 minute stroll to Worthing town centre. It is close to Beach House Park which each year is home the English Bowls Championship. If you're looking for a beautiful relaxing place to stay in Sussex, then the Park House is the place for you.* AA ★★★★

Tel & Fax: 01903 207939 • www.theparkhousehotel.com

Please note

Bedfordshire

Cambridgeshire

symbols

🚭	Totally non-smoking	🐕	Pets Welcome
🎠	Children Welcome	🌲	Christmas Breaks
♿	Suitable for Disabled Guests	♉	Licensed

Essex

Hertfordshire

FHG Guides
publish a large range of well-known accommodation guides.
We will be happy to send you details or you can use the order form
at the back of this book.

A useful index of towns/counties appears on pages 196-198

Norfolk

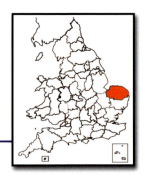

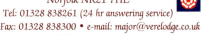

symbols

	Totally non-smoking		Pets Welcome
	Children Welcome		Christmas Breaks
	Suitable for Disabled Guests		Licensed

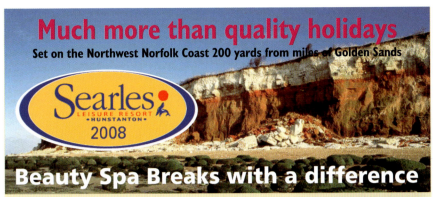

Much more than quality holidays

Set on the Northwest Norfolk Coast 200 yards from miles of Golden Sands

Beauty Spa Breaks with a difference

Our superb facilities are well equipped to provide relaxing, excellent value for money beauty spa breaks out of the school holidays & are ideal for a group of friends.

Reflections Hair and Beauty Salon at Searles

■ Included in Our Beauty Spa package are the following:
Unlimited use of the Indoor Pool, Sauna, Jacuzzi and Gymnasium.
Two days Half Board including Evening meals and Breakfast.
Full access to all of Searles superb leisure and entertainment facilities.

■ Our beauty breaks cost just £84 per person for 5 treatments, you just have to select the level of accommodation that is right for you

Accommodation

Searles accommodation is available in eight different ranges, from luxurious pine

Great savings on Short Breaks and Holidays – see website for special deals and offers

lodges to Classic Cabins, cosy Coastal Cottages, to the inviting Royal Range; we have something to suit all tastes.
Our Leisure Lodges, Prestige & Winchester Range represent real quality in terms of furniture, fixtures, size and setting, in fact all of the comforts of home with those special added extras to make any stay a real pleasure.

Suffolk

symbols

 Totally non-smoking 　　 Pets Welcome

Children Welcome 　　Christmas Breaks

 Suitable for Disabled Guests 　　Licensed

Derbyshire

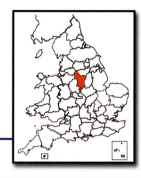

Dove Cottage, Church Lane, Mayfield, Ashbourne.
This modernised 200-year-old cottage in Mayfield village is ideally situated for shops, pubs, busy market towns, sporting facilities, lovely Dove Valley, Alton Towers, Peaks and Staffordshire Moorlands and many other places of interest. The cottage is comfortably furnished and well-equipped with TV, fridge, automatic washing machine, gas central heating. The fenced garden overlooks farmland. Sleeps seven. Garage and parking. Children welcome. Pets by arrangement. Available for long and short lets, also mid-week bookings. Price and brochure on request. Further details from:
Arthur Tatlow, Ashview, Ashfield Farm, Calwich, Ashbourne DE6 2EB Tel: 01335 324443 or 324279

THROWLEY HALL
FARM

- Self-catering accommodation in farmhouse for up to 12 and cottage for seven people (**ETC ★★★★**).
- Also Bed and Breakfast in farmhouse (**ETC ★★★★**).
Central heating, en suite rooms • No smoking TV, tea/coffee facilities in rooms • Children and pets welcome • Near Alton Towers and stately homes.

Details from Mrs M.A. Richardson, Throwley Hall Farm, Ilam, Near Ashbourne, Derbyshire DE6 2BB
Tel: 01538 308202/308243 • www.throwleyhallfarm.co.uk
e-mail: throwleyhall@talk21.com OR throwley@btinternet.com

◆ At almost 1000ft above sea level, the village nestles at the head of Lathkill Dale, a National Nature Reserve, and is surrounded by the stunning scenery of the White Peak.
◆ Cycle hire and fantastic horse riding are available locally.
◆ Clean and comfortable accommodation awaits you. Rooms (single, double and twin) with en suite facilities, tea/coffee, Sky TV, dvd player, radio and hairdryers and are centrally heated and double glazed. Laundry facilities are also available to guests.
◆ Varied and scrumptious Aga-cooked breakfasts are served daily
◆ Children and pets welcome by arrangement.
◆ Private parking ◆ Drive and Hike service.
◆ B&B from £25pppn
e-mail: rowsonfarm@btconnect.com
www.rowsonhousefarm.com

Rowson House Farm
Monyash, Bakewell DE45 1JH
Tel: 01629 813521

MONA VILLAS
**Church Lane
Middle Mayfield
Mayfield
Near Ashbourne
DE6 2JS**

Tel: 01335 343773

A warm, friendly welcome to our home with purpose-built en suite accommodation. Beautiful views over open countryside. A local pub serves excellent food within a five minute walk. Situated near Alton Towers, Dove Dale, etc. Three en suite rooms available, single supplement applies. Family rooms available. Parking.

Bed and Breakfast from £22.50 to £25.00 per night.

**e-mail: info@mona-villas.fsnet.co.uk
www.mona-villas.fsnet.co.uk**

Herefordshire

The Bridge at Wilton • Restaurant & Rooms

**Flavours of Herefordshire
Restaurant of the Year 2005/6/7**

Set in gardens which run down to the banks of the River Wye, this Georgian country house is an idyllic location to unwind and take a well deserved break. There are 8 beautifully appointed en suite bedrooms, several restaurant areas and adjoining bar and conservatory areas from which to enjoy the views across the river. The Restaurant attracts diners from around the country, with unique, exciting and truly imaginative dishes to savour and remember.

**The Bridge at Wilton, Ross-on-Wye HR9 6AA
Tel: 01989 562655 • Fax: 01989 567652**
e-mail: info@bridge-house-hotel.com • www.bridge-house-hotel.com

Please mention **Recommended Short Breaks**
when making enquiries about accommodation featured in these pages

Leicestershire & Rutland

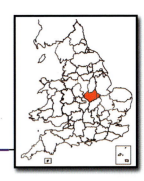

symbols

 Totally non-smoking

 Children Welcome

 Suitable for Disabled Guests

 Pets Welcome

 Christmas Breaks

 Licensed

HAMBLETON HALL
Hambleton, Oakham, Rutland LE15 8TH

The county of Rutland is verdant, undulating, and largely unspoilt, making it an ideal place to spend a tranquil vacation. No better venue for such an excursion exists than this fine hotel, perched in the very centre of man-made Rutland Water. The superb cuisine exhibits flair and refreshing originality, with the emphasis very much on seasonal, freshly sourced ingredients. Beautifully furnished in subtle shades, elegant and profoundly comfortable, with 17 individually and lavishly decorated bedrooms. Hambleton is within easy reach of numerous places of historic interest, wonderful gardens and antique shops. On-site tennis, outdoor heated swimming pool and croquet lawn, and within a short drive, horse riding, golf, sailing, fishing and boating.

Tel: 01572 756991
Fax: 01572 724721
hotel@hambletonhall.com
www.hambletonhall.com

Lincolnshire

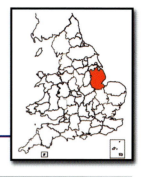

Two pine log cabins in peaceful woodland setting offering a relaxing holiday, ideally situated for the Wolds and the beautiful city of Lincoln.
Each has three bedrooms, one double, one twin, one child's bunkbed; large lounge, bathroom, kitchen, large veranda. Gas central heating, gas cooking. Car parking by unit. Near bus route. Linen provided. Pick up from Lincoln or Market Rasen Station available.

Terms £200 to £400 per week, £100 to £200 per 3-day stay.
Complimentary local food hamper.
Visit our website or ask for a brochure.

Mr R. Cox, Lincolnshire Lanes Log Cabins,
Manor Farm, East Firsby, Market Rasen LN8 2DB
Tel: 01673 878258
e-mail: info@lincolnshire-lanes.com
www.lincolnshire-lanes.com

PETWOOD
HOTEL

Stixwould Road, Woodhall Spa LN10 6QG
Tel: 01526 352411 • Fax: 01526 353473
reception@petwood.co.uk • www.petwood.co.uk

Originally built in the early 1900s The Petwood Hotel stands in 30 acres of mature woodland and gardens. During World War II, 617 Squadron, known as the "Dambusters", used the hotel as their Officers' Mess. Today it is a country house hotel of unique charm, offering a high standard of comfort and hospitality in elegant surroundings. All bedrooms are fully equipped to meet the needs of today's discerning guests, and the highly recommended Tennysons Restaurant offers the very best of English and Continental cuisine. There are ample leisure opportunities available locally as well as tranquil villages and historic market towns to explore.

AA ★★★ ETC

Village Limits Motel & Restaurant Woodhall Spa Lincs LN10 6UJ
Tel: 01526 353312 • www.villagelimits.co.uk

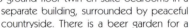

Under new management, the Village Limits Freehouse in Woodhall Spa is a thriving business. The new owners pride themselves on offering comfortable, high standard B&B accommodation beside their restaurant. There are 8 ground floor twin en suite bedrooms in a

separate building, surrounded by peaceful countryside. There is a beer garden for a relaxing drink, with stunning views of the Lincolnshire countryside. The restaurant serves freshly prepared British food using local ingredients wherever possible. There is an à la carte menu Tues-Sun 12-2pm and 7-9pm (Sunday lunch is a set menu), and a regularly updated specials board. *We hope to see you soon.*

FHG Guides

publish a large range of well-known accommodation guides.
We will be happy to send you details or you can use the order form
at the back of this book.

Northamptonshire

Spanhoe Lodge

Laxton, Rockingham Forest, Northants NN17 3AT

Steve & Jennie offer superb, friendly accommodation in a quiet and pretty rural location. Our 12 rooms (8 new) are well appointed with large en suite bathrooms. All rooms have TV, video and a full hospitality tray. For disabled guests, one of our rooms has direct access (through French doors) from the parking area via a gently sloping ramp. Fully enabled room with wheel-in wet area and aids. Ideal for families are our connecting rooms which give parents peace and privacy whilst having the children close at hand. Many excellent walks start here at Spanhoe Lodge, including the well known Jurassic Way. Packed lunches are always available. Strictly non-smoking. Bar and Small Restaurant Award 2008.

Tel: 01780 450328 • www.spanhoelodge.co.uk

Visit the FHG website
www.holidayguides.com
for details of the wide choice of accommodation
featured in the full range of FHG titles

symbols

 Totally non-smoking　　 Pets Welcome

 Children Welcome　　 Christmas Breaks

 Suitable for Disabled Guests　　 Licensed

Shropshire

Put your feet up and relax in the recliners as the beauty of the garden and the views of Clun and its surrounding hills provide solace from the stress of modern day life. Receive a warm welcome at this traditional oak-beamed farmhouse set back from the working farm. Two bedrooms, double en suite or double/family with private bathroom, tea/coffee facilities and good home cooking. Visitors' lounge with inglenook fireplace; separate dining room. Walks, history and attractions all close by.

Llanhedric

Bed and Breakfast from £25. Reductions for children.
Non-smoking household. Regret no dogs in house.
Open April to October.

Mrs M. Jones, Llanhedric, Clun, Craven Arms SY7 8NG • 01588 640203

Hazel Cottage • Duxmoor • Onibury, Craven Arms

Beautifully restored, semi-detached, yet private, period cottage, set in its own extensive cottage-style garden with its own drive and ample parking space. Amidst peaceful surroundings and panoramic views of the countryside, it is situated five miles north of historic Ludlow and one-and-a-half miles from the A49. The cottage retains all its original features and fittings with traditional decoration and is fully furnished, with antiques throughout. It comprises a comfortable living room with a Victorian range for coal and log fire; TV, wireless and telephone; dining room with bread oven; fully equipped kitchen, hall, Victorian bathroom; two bedrooms (one double and one twin-bedded) with period washbasins. Electric central heating throughout. All linen included. Tourist information. Open all year. No pets.

Terms from £205 to £440 per week • Short Breaks available

Mrs Rachel Sanders, Duxmoor Farm, Onibury, Craven Arms SY7 9BQ
01584 856342 • e-mail: rachelsanders@mac.com • www.stmem.com/hazelcottage

Mocktree Barns Holiday Cottages
'Best Value for Money' Gold Award 2006

A small group of comfortable self-catering cottages around a sunny courtyard. Well-equipped. Sleeping 2-6. Two cottages with no stairs. Friendly owners. Open all year. Short breaks. Pets and children welcome. Lovely views. Excellent walks from the door through farmland and woods. Hereford, Cider Country, Black & White villages, Shropshire Hills, Shrewsbury, and Ironbridge all an easy drive. Beautiful Ludlow seven miles. Good food and drink nearby. Brochure available.

Clive and Cynthia Prior, Mocktree Barns, Leintwardine, Ludlow SY7 0LY
Tel: 01547 540441 • e-mail: mocktreebarns@care4free.net
www.mocktreeholidays.co.uk

VisitBritain
★★★

Staffordshire

Warwickshire

Please note

All the information in this book is given in good faith in the belief that it is correct. However, the publishers cannot guarantee the facts given in these pages, neither are they responsible for changes in policy, ownership or terms that may take place after the date of going to press. Readers should always satisfy themselves that the facilities they require are available and that the terms, if quoted, still apply.

Terms quoted in this publication may be subject to increase if rises in costs necessitate

Worcestershire

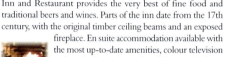

East Yorkshire

North Yorkshire

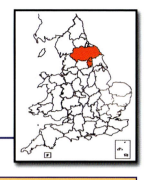

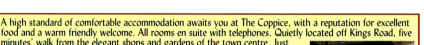

BAYTREE HOUSE

98 Franklin Road, Harrogate HG1 5EN
Tel: 01423 564493
e-mail: info@baytreeharrogate.co.uk
www.baytreeharrogate.co.uk

On a quiet, tree-lined avenue, we provide high quality bed and breakfast for visitors taking short breaks and business trips in Harrogate, in the heart of Yorkshire. The attractions of the Yorkshire Dales and Moors are all close at hand, and Harrogate itself has many attractions for the visitor.

All rooms are en suite, with luxury touches to make your stay really comfortable. Our breakfast menus use only the finest award-winning local produce. This is a non-smoking establishment. Off-street parking available. Parties welcome. *International Conference Centre less than 5 minutes' stroll away.*

Experience the unique atmosphere and traditional hospitality at...

SIMONSTONE HALL

Set in magnificent countryside near the market town of Hawes, Simonstone Hall is a beautifully restored country house hotel with spectacular views over the dale and surrounding fell.
• Outstanding Bar Meals and Sunday Lunches served in the Game Tavern and Orangery, our Restaurant provides an elegant setting for our wide selection of fine foods and wines.
• An excellent base for walking and exploring the Dales.
• Pets welcome in most rooms.
A relaxed, friendly establishment with open fires, four-poster beds and experienced staff to look after all your needs.

Simonstone Hall, Hawes, North Yorkshire DL8 3LY

Telephone: 01969 667255 • Fax: 01969 667741
e-mail: email@simonstonehall.demon.co.uk
www.simonstonehall.co.uk   AA ★★

The INN at Hawnby

ETC ★★★★

Hilltop, Hawnby, Helmsley, York YO62 5QS
•Tel: 01439 798202 •Fax: 01439 798344
•info@innathawnby.co.uk •www.innathawnby.co.uk

The Inn at Hawnby is set in the heart of the North York Moors National Park, offering spectacular views from its hilltop location. Comfortable country decor has been chosen to create nine attractive en suite bedrooms which have telephones, televisions, ironing facilities, hairdryers, and tea and coffee trays. There is easy access for hiking, climbing, horse riding, hang gliding, and free fishing on the River Seph. Historic sites such as Rievaulx Abbey, Duncombe Park and Castle Howard are nearby, as is the wonderful city of York.

The Inn at Hawnby offers warm, relaxing breaks at any time of the year. Fully licensed.

---

symbols

 Totally non-smoking   Pets Welcome

 Children Welcome   Christmas Breaks

 Suitable for Disabled Guests   Licensed

Mowbray Stable Cottages
Stockton Road, South Kilvington YO7 2LY
Mrs M. Backhouse - 01845 522605

Situated within a mile of Thirsk and the village of South Kilvington, these recently converted cottages provide an ideal base for exploring the North Yorkshire Moors, Yorkshire Dales, and within easy reach of York, Durham, and the east coast. **COTTAGE NO. 1** sleeps four. One double bedroom, one twin, a large shower room, combined living/kitchen/dining room. Ramped access for wheelchairs, wider doors throughout, handrails etc. in shower room. **COTTAGE NO. 2** sleeps two. One double bedroom, en suite shower room, living room, separate kitchen/dining room. Not suitable for wheelchair users. Both cottages are equipped with an electric oven/hob, fridge, microwave, colour TV, shaver point and gas central heating. Linen, but not towels, are included in price. Pets welcome by arrangement. Car essential. No smoking.

Cottage No.1 £50 per night • Cottage No.2 £35 per night • Min. 2 nights

www.greenhouses-farm-cottages.co.uk

Set in the tiny hamlet of Greenhouses and enjoying splendid views over open countryside, three cottages offering a very quiet and peaceful setting for a holiday. The cottages have been converted from the traditional farm buildings and the olde world character has been retained in the thick stone walls, exposed beams and red pantile roofs. All are well equipped, and linen, fuel and lighting are included in the price. There are ample safe areas for children to play. **Sorry, no pets. Prices from £225 to £600 per week. Winter Breaks from £175.**

Nick Eddleston, Greenhouses Farm Cottages, Greenhouses Farm, Lealholm, Near Whitby YO21 2AD • 01947 897486

Set in a Georgian townhouse on a leafy avenue, a warm welcome awaits at our friendly, family-run guest house. Located only minutes' walk from the historic Bar Walls and York Minster, restaurants, bars and shopping, we are in

Blossoms
York

an ideal location for exploring York. We pride ourselves on offering a good service combined with value-for-money prices.

All rooms are recently decorated and en suite with WC and shower; TV, tea tray and phone. Family rooms for up to 6 people. Bar and lounge. Free internet access and wi-fi. Free car park. Local information available.

Sun-Thurs from £22.50pp • Fri and Sat from £30pp
3-night midweek spring and autumn specials from £20pp
See our website for latest prices and offers

Tel: 01904 652391
Fax: 01904 652392
e-mail: fhg@blossomsyork.co.uk

www.blossomsyork.co.uk.

Newton House

Diana and John offer all their guests a friendly and warm welcome to their Victorian end town house a few minutes' walk from the city centre, York's beautiful Minster, medieval walls and museums. We are only a 40 mile drive from coastal resorts, the lovely Yorkshire Moors and Dales. Three double/twin en suite rooms, colour TV, tea/coffee tray, central heating. Breakfast menu. Car park. NON-SMOKING. Fire Certificate. Terms from £26pp.

Newton House, Neville Street, Haxby Road, York YO31 8NP • 01904 635627

South Yorkshire

An ideal location to spend time with your horse, mountain bike or walking boots. Two comfortably furnished cottages attached to main stable building (each sleeps 6/8). Well equipped, bed linen provided. Non-smoking. Dogs not allowed, but kennels available.

Pennine Equine Holiday Cottages
Cote Green Farm, Wortley

Livery and stabling for visitors' horses. 3-mile cross country course within grounds. Riding lessons available. Ample parking for trailers, horse boxes etc.

Bromley Farm, Wortley, Sheffield S35 7DE
Tel: 0114 284 7140
or 07939 906523
www.pennine-equine.co.uk

FREE or REDUCED RATE entry to Holiday Visits and Attractions – see our **READERS' OFFER VOUCHERS** on pages 199-206

West Yorkshire

Please note

All the information in this book is given in good faith in the belief that it is correct. However, the
publishers cannot guarantee the facts given in these pages, neither are they responsible for
changes in policy, ownership or terms that may take place after the date of going to press. Readers
should always satisfy themselves that the facilities they require are available
and that the terms, if quoted, still apply.

Visit the FHG website

www.holidayguides.com

for details of the wide choice of accommodation

featured in the full range of FHG titles

Durham

Publisher's note

While every effort is made to ensure accuracy, we regret that FHG Guides cannot accept responsibility for errors, misrepresentations or omissions in our entries or any consequences thereof. Prices in particular should be checked.
We will follow up complaints but cannot act as arbiters or agents for either party.

Northumberland

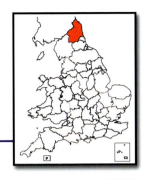

Cheshire

Chester & Cheshire

Soak in the atmosphere of the historic city of Chester, created by an abundance of black & white buildings set in a circuit of glorious city walls, the most complete in the country. Chester's crowning glory is the 13th century Rows – two tiers of shops running along the main streets, offering a unique and sophisticated shopping experience.

A leisurely walk along the finest city walls in Britain will take you past most of the city's delights like the stunning Eastgate Clock and the 1000-year-old Cathedral, a haven of reflective tranquillity in a lively, bustling, cosmopolitan centre. The biggest archaeological dig in Britain is currently underway at the 2000-year-old Roman Amphitheatre; there is architectural splendour to enjoy at every turn.

The lush countryside surrounding Chester is peppered with stately homes, award-winning gardens and chic market towns featuring characteristic black and white half-timbered buildings.

Tatton Park near Knutsford is one of Britain's finest Georgian manors, with acres of parklands and formal gardens, a perfect attraction to enjoy in every season, and the host of the RHS Flower Show in July. Or Arley Hall and Gardens near Northwich, with its stunning herbaceous borders and Country Fair and Horse Trials in May.

For super chic in super villages and towns, breeze into Tarporley, Nantwich, Knutsford and Wilmslow where sophisticated shopping, fine cuisine and contemporary pleasures ensure an afternoon of indulgence and fine delights, with food and drink festivals being held throughout the year.

To discover Chester and Cheshire, simply visitchester.com

symbols

 Totally non-smoking

 Children Welcome

 Suitable for Disabled Guests

 Pets Welcome

 Christmas Breaks

 Licensed

Cumbria

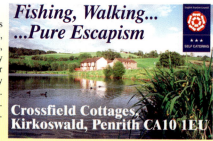

symbols

	Totally non-smoking		Pets Welcome
	Children Welcome		Christmas Breaks
	Suitable for Disabled Guests		Licensed

THE FAMOUS

WILD BOAR

"Tucked away amongst the gently rolling countryside and quiet Gilpin Valley, with 72 acres of its own private woodland, this former coaching inn is famed for its traditional atmosphere and the warmth of its welcome."

Complementing the hotel perfectly, bedrooms are cosy and comfortable, and the restaurant offers a menu that makes the very most of Lakeland produce, accompanied by an extensive wine list.

THE FAMOUS WILD BOAR
Crook, Near Windermere
Cumbria LA23 3NF
RESERVATIONS: 08458 504604
www.elh.co.uk

English Lakes Hotels

Lancashire

FHG Guides

publish a large range of well-known accommodation guides.
We will be happy to send you details or you can use the order form
at the back of this book.

Looking for Holiday
Accommodation?

for details of hundreds of properties throughout the UK, visit our website

www.holidayguides.com

Scotland · Regions

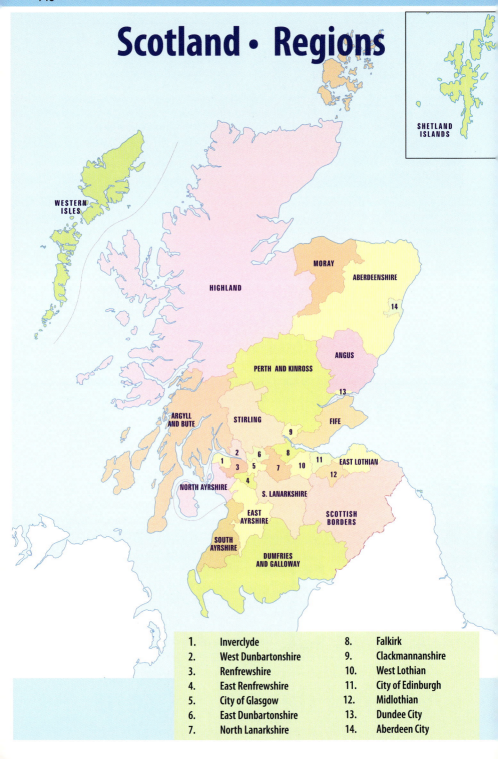

SHETLAND
ISLANDS

WESTERN
ISLES

MORAY

ABERDEENSHIRE

HIGHLAND

14

ANGUS

PERTH AND KINROSS

13

ARGYLL
AND BUTE

STIRLING

FIFE

9

2

6

8

1

5

11

EAST LOTHIAN

3

7

10

4

12

NORTH AYRSHIRE

S. LANARKSHIRE

EAST
AYRSHIRE

SCOTTISH
BORDERS

SOUTH
AYRSHIRE

DUMFRIES
AND GALLOWAY

1.	Inverclyde	8.	Falkirk
2.	West Dunbartonshire	9.	Clackmannanshire
3.	Renfrewshire	10.	West Lothian
4.	East Renfrewshire	11.	City of Edinburgh
5.	City of Glasgow	12.	Midlothian
6.	East Dunbartonshire	13.	Dundee City
7.	North Lanarkshire	14.	Aberdeen City

Scotland

Scotland

photo supplied by VisitScotland Aberdeen & Grampian

THE HIGHLANDS AND ISLANDS include much of what is often thought of as the 'real' Scotland. Stretching north from Fort William and Ben Nevis in the west to Inverness and the Moray Firth in the east, this unspoiled area contains some of Britain's most remote, least populated and most beautiful districts. The North West Highlands is the first area of Scotland to be awarded UNESCO-endorsed European Geopark status. The area which encompasses parts of Wester Ross and the whole of North West Sutherland has been designated as a Geopark on the basis of its outstanding geology and landscape, the strength of its partnership approach to sustainable economic development and its existing geological interpretation.

On the eastern borders of the Highlands lie Aberdeenshire and Moray, with their rugged peaks and rolling farmlands. Rich in fish, whisky, oil and castles, these counties boast 'Royal' Deeside, with Braemar and Balmoral as a tourist 'honeypot' and share with their neighbouring counties some of the most impressive scenery in Britain. Perth

& Kinross and Angus offer a wealth of leisure activities: ski-ing in the glens, fishing on Loch Leven or Loch Earn, golf at Gleneagles or Carnoustie, climbing Lochnagar, pony trekking round Loch Tay, or sea-bathing at Arbroath or Montrose. The many attractive towns like Pitlochry, Aberfeldy, Crieff, Forfar etc and the busy cities of Perth and Dundee offer civilised shopping, eating and accommodation facilities.

Convenient road, rail and air links make Central and South-West Scotland a popular tourist destination. Argyll has a long, much indented coastline, looking out onto a scatter of islands such as Mull, Jura, Gigha and Islay. This is a popular outdoor resort area and has excellent hotels and a wide choice of self catering accommodation. Oban is the principal centre and a busy port for the Inner and Outer Hebrides. The lively city of Glasgow is well worth a visit and has a growing reputation for its superb cultural, entertainment, shopping and sporting facilities. Ayrshire naturally means Rabbie Bums and Alloway, and also means golf – Prestwick, Troon and Turnberry are courses of international renown. Make time for a trip across to the lovely Isle of Arran – 'Scotland in miniature'.

Central Scotland is surprisingly rich in scenery and historic interest. The 'bonnie banks' of Loch Lomond, the Trossachs, Stirling Castle and Bannockburn are just some of the treasure stored here in the heart of Scotland. Excellent holiday centres with plenty of accommodation include Stirling itself, Killin, Aberfoyle, Callander, Lochearnhead and Dunblane. The rolling hills and fields of the Lothians, with Edinburgh at the heart, sweep down to the Forth as it enters the North Sea.

Edinburgh is the country's capital and a year-round tourist destination. It is always full of interest – the castle, the Palace of Holyrood, museums, galleries, pubs and entertainment. North Berwick and Dunbar are popular coastal resorts and this area, like Fife and Ayrshire, is a golfers' paradise. Opening onto the sea between the Lothians and Berwick-on-Tweed (which is technically in England), are the very attractive Scottish Borders. The ruined abbeys of Dryburgh, Jedburgh, Kelso and Melrose are a main attraction, as are the mills and mill-shops for the woollens which have made towns like Hawick and Galashiels famous.

A short break in St Andrews and the Kingdom of Fife is the ideal escape from the pressures of everyday life. Curl up in a comfy chair by a roaring fire in an ancient castle hotel. Sample superb cuisine in gracious surroundings in a stately home. Or treat the family to a self-catering break in a house with a view. And no matter what time of year you choose to come, you can be sure that there will be plenty of things to see and do. With its dry climate, most sports, including golf, can be played throughout the year. And as the scenery changes character with each season, you will notice something new no matter how many times you return. It is, of course, golf that has placed Fife on the world stage. St Andrews is the "Home of Golf", and the town, and Fife in general, boasts many fine courses which can be played all year round.

For walkers, the Southern Upland Way runs from Cockburnpath on the east coast, through the Borders to Portpatrick, near Stranraer from where ferry services leave for Northern Ireland. We are now in Dumfries & Galloway whose hills and valleys run down to the Solway Firth within sight of the English Lake District. This is a popular touring and holiday region, with its green and fertile countryside, pleasant small towns and villages, and many attractions to visit.

www.visitscotland.com

Scotland
Great Days Out: Visits and Attractions

Culzean Castle and Country Park
Maybole, Ayrshire • 0870 118 1945
www.culzeanexperience.org
Robert Adam's masterpiece set in beautifully landscaped gardens. Investigate the Eisenhower connection and visit the Interpretation Centre, swan pond and aviary. Restaurant and tea rooms, picnic areas.

Creetown Gemrock Museum
Newton Stewart • 01671 820357
www.gemrock.net
Gems, crystals, rocks and fossils from all over the world, many displayed in a realistic cave setting; 'Fire in the Stones' AV presentation; tearoom and internet cafe.

Kelvingrove Art Gallery & Museum
Glasgow • 0141-276 9599
www.glasgowmuseums.com
An adventure through art, time and the natural world brought to life, with film, sound and computer activities in Glasgow's newly restored museum and art gallery.

Scotland's Secret Bunker
Near St Andrews, Fife • 01333 310301
www.secretbunker.co.uk
An amazing labyrinth built 100ft below ground, from where the country would have been run in the event of nuclear war. The command centre with its original equipment can be seen, AV theatre and two cinemas.

Sensation Science Centre
Dundee • 01382 228800
www.sensation.org.uk
A unique 4-star visitor attraction devoted to the five senses, with over 60 hands-on exhibits, live science shows and workshops.

Castle & Gardens of Mey
Near Thurso • 01847 851473
www.castleofmey.org.uk
The most northerly castle on the British mainland, renovated and restored by the late Queen Mother. Beautiful gardens with views across the Pentland Firth to Orkney.

The Loch Ness Monster Visitor Centre
Drumnadrochit, Inverness • 01456 450342
www.lochness-centre.com
All you ever wanted to know about the monster! Superb documentary, including eye-witness accounts. Shop with souvenirs.

Inverewe Gardens
Poolewe • 0844 493 2225
www.nts.org.uk
At a latitude more northerly than Moscow, the warm currents of the Gulf Stream have created an oasis of colour and fertility, where exotic plants flourish. Visitor centre and restaurant.

Our Dynamic Earth
Edinburgh • 0131 550 7800
www.dynamicearth.co.uk
Charting the Earth's progress and development over the last 4500 million years, with plenty of interactive entertainment to fascinate all ages. Gift shop and cafe.

Scottish Mining Museum
Newtongrange, Midlothian • 0131- 663 7519
www.scottishminingmuseum.com
Ex-miners take you on a tour of Scotland's most famous colliery, award winning talking tableaux, audio-visual presentation and new life-size reconstruction of coal-face. Tearoom.

Scone Palace
Perth •01738 552300
www.scone-palace.net
With a history stretching back 1500 years, this has been the seat of parliaments and the crowning place of kings. It is a treasury of furniture, paintings, porcelain and objets d'art. Adventure playground and maze.

The Falkirk Wheel
Falkirk, Stirlingshire • 08700 500 208
www.thefalkirkwheel.co.uk
Measuring 115ft. the world's only rotating boatlift links the Forth & Clyde and Union Canals using state-of-the-art engineering. Visitor centre and boat trips.

Ladyglen Hotels

Hetland Hall Hotel
Carrutherstown
Dumfries
DG1 4JX
Tel: 01387 840201
Fax: 01387 840211
info@hetlandhallhotel.co.uk
www.hetlandhallhotel.co.uk

King Robert Hotel
Glasgow Road
Bannockburn
Stirling FK7 0LJ
Tel: 01786 811666
Fax: 01786 811507
info@kingroberthotel.co.uk
www.kingroberthotel.co.uk

Rob Roy Hotel
Aberfoyle
Stirlingshire
FK8 3UX
Tel: 01877 382245
Fax: 01877 382262
info@robroyhotel.co.uk
www.robroyhotel.co.uk

Publisher's note

While every effort is made to ensure accuracy, we regret that FHG Guides cannot accept responsibility for errors, misrepresentations or omissions in our entries or any consequences thereof. Prices in particular should be checked.

We will follow up complaints but cannot act as arbiters or agents for either party.

Aberdeen, Banff & Moray

Macdonald Pittodrie House

One of Scotland's most historic and picturesque hotels, originally built in 1480, still stands amidst the 2500 acre Pittodrie estate, nestling at the foot of the spectacular Bennachie. Stunning views, extensive private gardens and a reputation for culinary excellence and impecccable service combine to ensure your stay will be perfect in every way.

Turrets, spiral staircases, period furniture and ancestral portraits
Make yourself at home in our comfortable surroundings. Dining Room, Drawing Room, Orangery and Patio, Library, Billiard Room, Ballroom, Snug Bar. Log fires in winter, Victorian walled garden.

Luxury accommodation in each unique bedroom
27 rooms/suites, all with private facilities, radio, satellite television, direct dial telephone, wireless broadband internet access, trouser press, iron and ironing board, tea & coffee making facilities, hairdryer, dressing gown and slippers; newspaper deliveries, laundry and dry-cleaning service.

An impressive range of activities around the Estate
Individually tailored – from purely social to teambuilding, from a couple of hours to a whole day, including off-road driving, clay pigeon shooting, archery, shooting, quad-biking, one-man hovercraft, fly casting, family fun days.
Golf, fishing and deer stalking available locally. Also several interesting walks around the Pittodrie estate.

Savour the taste of Scottish country house cooking
Food and drink of the very highest quality in "The Mither Tap" Restaurant, prepared by our award-winning chef, incorporating the freshest of seasonal ingredients. Exceptional international list of over 200 wines, and over 140 malt whiskies on offer in the bar.

Wedding, Conference and Banqueting facilities
Full of period character, and with Bennachie as a backdrop, Pittodrie House is the perfect setting for a truly romantic wedding. Call our management team on **01467 681 744** and arrange to look round the hotel and experience the facilities.

MACDONALD
PITTODRIE HOUSE
Chapel of Garioch, Near Inverurie, Aberdeenshire AB51 5HS
Tel: 01467 681744 • Fax: 01467 681648 • E-mail: pittodrie@macdonald-hotels.co.uk

www.macdonaldhotels.co.uk/pittodrie

Angus & Dundee

Lochside Lodge & Roundhouse Restaurant

A converted farm steading, Lochside Lodge is set in the midst of the most picturesque of the Angus Glens, with a huge choice of things to see and do. The hay loft of the steading has been converted into a number of well appointed rooms, including a family room, all en suite, with TV, tea and coffee making facilities, and bathrobes. In addition, two courtyard bedrooms offer ground floor access.

The best of local produce awaits you in the bar or restaurant, prepared by Graham Riley, Master Chef of Great Britain. Winner of many awards, the lunch and dinner menus change on a regular basis.

**Bridgend of Lintrathen, Kirriemuir, Angus DD8 5JJ • Tel: 01575 560340
Fax: 01575 560202 • e-mail: enquiries@lochsidelodge.com • www.lochsidelodge.com**

**Glen Clova Hotel, Glen Clova, Near Kirriemuir DD8 4QS • Tel: 01575 550350
Fax: 01575 550292 • e-mail: Hotel@clova.com • www.clova.com**

Set in an area of oustanding natural beauty and botanical interest, Glen Clova has something to offer everyone. Be our guest and live *The Real Scottish Experience.*

• All bedrooms with full en suite facilities, courtesy trays and TV.

• The Steading Bunkhouse provides basic but functional self-catering accommodation for the true outdoor type.

• Cadam & Kirkton luxury wooden lodges, sleep up to 6 each, both with saunas and hot tubs.

• Climbers' Bar with a lively atmosphere, fine cask ales and a roaring fire in winter; Lounge Bar and Conservatory offer comfortable, informal surroundings for relaxation.

symbols

Totally non-smoking	Pets Welcome	
Children Welcome	Christmas Breaks	
Suitable for Disabled Guests	Licensed	

Argyll & Bute

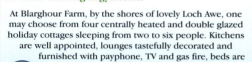

Situated in the Inner Hebrides, the community owned Isle of Gigha (God's Island) is surely one of Scotland's most beautiful and tranquil islands. Explore the white sandy bays and lochs. Easy walking, bike hire, birds, wildlife and wild flowers. Home to the famous Achamore Gardens with rhododendrons, azaleas and semi-tropical plants. Grass Airstrip, 9-hole golf course and regular ferry (only 20 minutes from the mainland). We are dog friendly. Holiday Cottages also available.

Call us on **01583 505254** Fax: 01583 505244 **www.gigha.org.uk**

Want a little time alone with that special someone???
Then come to Melfort Pier & Harbour!
Have your own house, with sauna, spa bath, two TVs, log fire, right on the shores of Loch Melfort. Some with sunbeds! Restaurant on site. Wi-fi.
Superb hill walking and fishing, nearby golf and gardens, shooting, shopping, ideal touring base.
Pets very welcome! • Min 2 nights • Start any day • Incl. all linen, electricity etc • Open all year

www.mellowmelfort.com
Remember to mention this advert for free use of canoe, free fishing, free firewood.
CALL FOR SPECIAL PROMOTIONS • PRICES FROM £90.00 – £225.00 PER HOUSE/NIGHT

MELFORT PIER & HARBOUR, Kilmelford, By Oban, Argyll PA34 4XD
Tel: **01852 200333** • e-mail: melharbour@aol.com

Visit the FHG website
www.holidayguides.com
for details of the wide choice of accommodation
featured in the full range of FHG titles

---

symbols

  Totally non-smoking   Pets Welcome

  Children Welcome   Christmas Breaks

  Suitable for Disabled Guests   Licensed

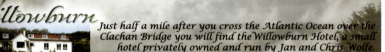

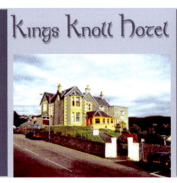

FHG Guides

publish a large range of well-known accommodation guides.
We will be happy to send you details or you can use the order form
at the back of this book.

A useful index of towns/counties appears on pages 196-198

Ayrshire & Arran

symbols

 Totally non-smoking

 Pets Welcome

 Children Welcome

 Christmas Breaks

 Suitable for Disabled Guests

 Licensed

Borders

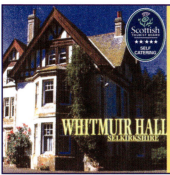

Dumfries & Galloway

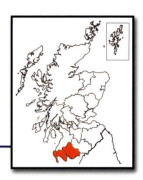

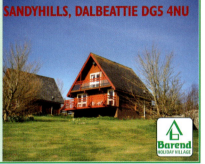

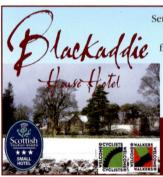
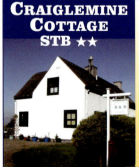

Edinburgh & Lothians

EDINBURGH & LOTHIANS

Scotland's Capital is home to a wide range of attractions offering something to visitors of all ages.
The annual Festival in August is part of the city's tradition and visitors flock to enjoy the performing
arts, theatre, ballet, cinema and music, and of course "The Tattoo" itself. Other festivals and enter-
tainments take place throughout the year, including children's festivals, science festivals, the famous Royal Highland Show and the Hogmanay street party.

East Lothian has beautiful countryside and dramatic coastline, all only a short distance from Edinburgh. Once thriving fishing villages, North Berwick and Dunbar now cater for visitors who delight
in their traditional seaside charm. In Midlothian you can step back in time with a visit to Rosslyn
Chapel or Borthwick and Crichton Castles, all dating from the 15th century, or seize the chance to
brush up on your swing at Melville Golf Range and Course.

Fife

symbols

 Totally non-smoking

 Pets Welcome

 Children Welcome

 Christmas Breaks

 Suitable for Disabled Guests

 Licensed

Highlands

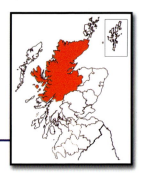

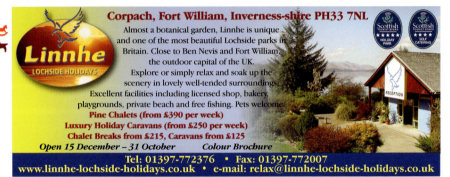

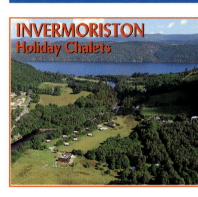

Lanarkshire

Perth & Kinross

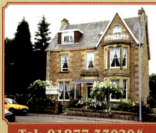

Stirling & The Trossachs

Riverview House

Leny Road, Callander FK17 8AL
Tel: 01877 330635

Excellent accommodation in the Trossachs area which forms the most beautiful part of Scotland's first National Park. Ideal centre for walking and cycling holidays, with cycle storage available. In the guest house all rooms are en suite, with TV and tea-making. Private parking. Also available self-catering stone cottages, sleep 3 or 4. Sorry, no smoking and no pets. Call Drew or Kathleen Little for details.

e-mail: drew@visitcallander.co.uk
www.visitcallander.co.uk

B&B from £26.
Low season and long stay discounts available.
Self-catering cottages from £150 per week
(STB 3 & 4 Stars).

Croftburn Bed & Breakfast
Croftamie, Drymen,
Loch Lomond G63 0HA

Dorothy and John Reid welcome you to Croftburn overlooking the Campsie Hills. Ideal for touring, walking, golf and fishing. 30 minutes from Glasgow and Stirling; convenient stopover on West Highland Way, Rob Roy Way and National Cycle Route.

All room with colour TV, hairdryer, and hospitality tray • Ample parking
En suite facilities available • Open all year

e-mail: johnreid@croftburn.fsnet.co.uk • www.croftburn.co.uk
Tel: 01360 660796 • Fax: 01360 661005

symbols

 Totally non-smoking
 Children Welcome
 Suitable for Disabled Guests

 Pets Welcome
 Christmas Breaks
 Licensed

Scottish Islands

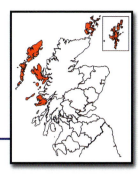

Set overlooking the picturesque harbour of Portree, The Royal Hotel offers you a quiet, relaxing retreat during your stay on Skye. Accommodation consists of 21 well appointed rooms, most overlooking the harbour and featuring private bathroom facilities and colour TV. Room service is available as well as a fitness centre and sauna for guests to use. The Royal Hotel offers a wide and varied menu serving sea food, lamb, venison and tender Highland beef. Vegetarians are also catered for. There is something for everyone, from walking, climbing and watersports to good food, great local arts & crafts, colourful museums and places of interest.

THE ROYAL HOTEL • Portree, Isle of Skye IV51 9BU
Tel: 01478 612525 • Fax: 01478 613198
e-mail: info@royal-hotel-skye.com • www.royal-hotel-skye.com

Toravaig House Hotel

Winner of the 'Scottish Island Hotel of the Year' 2005, 2007 -Hotel Review Scotland
Winner Conde Nast Johansens 'Most Excellent Service UK' Award 2006.
EatScotland Silver Award 2007

A stylish, elegant Country House Hotel with contemporary flair, Toravaig House has 9 beautifully presented en suite bedrooms with brass or sleigh beds, Sky TV, telephone, top quality showers and baths.

'Simply stylish...simply unique'

The Iona Restaurant (28 covers) serves fresh local dishes, including great sea food, game, and the best of Island produce. There is a good selection of fine wines from distant shores, and malt whisky from all around the Highlands. The hotel is set in two acres and enjoys fine views out to the mainland hills of Knoydart over the Sound of Sleat.
New for 2006, we offer daily yachting trips on the private hotel yacht. See our website for full details.

Knock Bay, Sleat, Isle of Skye IV44 8RE • Double/twin from £70pppn
Tel: 01471 820200 • Tel & Fax: 01471 833231 • info@skyehotel.co.uk • www.skyehotel.co.uk

Ratings & Awards

For the first time ever the AA, VisitBritain, VisitScotland, and the Wales Tourist Board will use a single method of assessing and rating serviced accommodation. Irrespective of which organisation inspects an establishment the rating awarded will be the same, using a common set of standards, giving a clear guide of what to expect. The RAC is no longer operating an Hotel inspection and accreditation business.

Accommodation Standards: Star Grading Scheme

Using a scale of 1-5 stars the objective quality ratings give a clear indication of accommodation standard, cleanliness, ambience, hospitality, service and food, This shows the full range of standards suitable for every budget and preference, and allows visitors to distinguish between the quality of accommodation and facilities on offer in different establishments. All types of board and self-catering accommodation are covered, including hotels,
B&Bs, holiday parks, campus accommodation, hostels, caravans and camping, and boats.

VisitBritain and the regional tourist boards, enjoyEngland.com, VisitScotland and VisitWales, and the AA have full details of the grading system on their websites

The more stars, the higher level of quality

★★★★★
exceptional quality, with a degree of luxury

★★★★
excellent standard throughout

★★★
very good level of quality and comfort

★★
good quality, well presented and well run

★
acceptable quality; simple, practical, no frills

National Accessible Scheme

If you have particular mobility, visual or hearing needs, look out for the National Accessible Scheme. You can be confident of finding accommodation or attractions that meet your needs by looking for the following symbols.

 Typically suitable for a person with sufficient mobility to climb a flight of steps but would benefit from fixtures and fittings to aid balance

 Typically suitable for a person with restricted walking ability and for those that may need to use a wheelchair some of the time and can negotiate a maximum of three steps

 Typically suitable for a person who depends on the use of a wheelchair and transfers unaided to and from the wheelchair in a seated position. This person may be an independent traveller

 Typically suitable for a person who depends on the use of a wheelchair in a seated position. This person also requires personal or mechanical assistance (eg carer, hoist).

Wales

SCENERY, history and the quality of life are the main ingredients of a holiday in Wales, which makes this a perfect destination for a holiday.

You can't go far in Wales without a view of mountains or the sea. And you can't go far in Wales without being in a National Park! Wales has three of these, each with its own special character. In the north, the Snowdonia National Park has mountains, moors, lakes and wooded valleys, dominated of course by Snowdon, the highest peak in England and Wales. At its northern edge is Anglesey and the North Wales Coast resorts, all popular tourist areas. But the atmosphere of the National Park is best experienced in the small towns and villages at its heart, such as Llanberis, Beddgelert, Betws-y-Coed and Capel Curig.

Approximately 100 km to the south and east is the Brecon Beacons National Park. From Llandeilo by the Black Mountain in the west, through the Brecon Beacons themselves to the Black Mountains and Hay-on-Wye on the border with England, here are grassy, smooth hills, open spaces, bare moors, lakes and forests. All that is lacking is the sea – and it's the sea which has made the Pembroke Coast National Park possible. From Tenby in the south to Cardigan in the north, the park offers every kind of coastal scenery: steep cliffs, sheltered bays and harbours, huge expanses of sand and shingle, rocky coves and quiet wooded inlets.

But 'scenery' doesn't end with the national parks. Wales also has five areas nominated officially as being of 'Outstanding Natural Beauty'. The Gower Peninsula, west of Swansea, is a scenic jewel – small but sparkling! The Wye Valley from Chepstow to Monmouth includes the ruined Tintern Abbey and many historic sites including Chepstow itself, Raglan and Caerleon.

The Isle of Anglesey, apart from its quiet beauty, claims the world's longest placename, usually shortened to Llanfair PG! The Llyn Peninsula, west of Snowdon is perhaps the most traditionally Welsh part of Wales and finally, the Clwydian Range behind Rhyl and Prestatyn, where St Asaph has the smallest cathedral in Britain.

www.visitwales.com

Wales
Great Days Out: Visits and Attractions

Bala Lake Railway
Llanuwchllyn• 01678 540666
www.bala-lake-railway.co.uk
A delightful 9-mile return journey alongside Bala Lake through Snowdonia National Park on a 2' narrow gauge steam railway.

Anglesey Sea Zoo
Brynsiencyn, Anglesey • 01248 430411
www.angleseyseazoo.co.uk
Meet the fascinating creatures that inhabit the sea and shores around Anglesey; adventure playground, shops and restaurant.

Ewe-phoria
Corwen, North Wales • 01490 460225
www.ewe-phoria.co.uk
Fascinating insight into the work of the shepherd and his sheepdog. Sheepdog and sheep shearing demonstrations, meet the lambs and puppies.

Sygun Copper Mine
Beddgelert, North Wales • 01766 890595
www.syguncoppermine.co.uk
Award-winning attraction with underground audio-visual tours. See stalagmites and stalactites formed from ferrous oxide.

Vale of Rheidol Railway
Aberystwyth, Ceredigion • 01970 625819
www.rheidolrailway.co.uk
An unforgettable journey by narrow gauge steam train, climbing over 600 feet in 12 miles from Aberystwyth to Devil's Bridge.There are many sharp turns and steep gradients, and the journey affords superb views of the valley.

The Animalarium
Borth, Ceredigion • 01970 871224
www.animalarium.co.uk
A collection of unusual and interesting animals. Get close to domestic and farm animals in the petting barn, and see exotic and endangered species in larger enclosures.

Pembroke Castle
Pembroke, Pembrokeshire • 01646 684585
www.pembroke-castle.co.uk
The birthplace of Henry VII, this is the oldest castle in West Wales, dating back to the 13th century, with a fine five-storey circular keep. Exhibitions, displays, videos and tableaux give a fascinating insight into history and heritage.

Manor House Wild Animal Park
Near Tenby, Pembrokeshire • 01646 651201
www.manorhousewildanimalpark.co.uk
Set in landscaped grounds round an 18th century manor. Lots of animals, including a 'close encounters' unit, plus daily falconry displays.

Powis Castle and Garden
Near Welshpool, Powys • 01938 551929
www.nationaltrust.org.uk
Perched on a rock above gardens of great historical and horticultural importance, the medieval castle contains a superb collection of paintings, furniture and treasures from India.

Centre for Alternative Technology
Machynlleth, Powys • 01654 705950
www.cat.org.uk
World-renowned centre demonstrating practical and sustainable solutions to modern problems. Water-powered cliff railway, dynamic displays of wind and solar power, and organic gardens.

Cefn Coed Colliery Museum
Neath, South Wales • 01639 750556
Housed in the buildings of what was once the deepest anthracite mine in the world, giving a vivid portrayal of the working conditions endured by the miners.

Caldicot Castle & Country Park
Near Chepstow • 01291 420241
www.caldicotcastle.co.uk
Explore the castle's fascinating past with an audio tour, and take in the breathtaking views of the 55-acre grounds from the battlements. Children's activity centre, play area; tearoom.

BRYN BRAS CASTLE

Llanrug, Near Caernarfon, Gwynedd LL55 4RE
Tel & Fax: (01286) 870210
e-mail: holidays@brynbrascastle.co.uk
www.brynbrascastle.co.uk

★★★★★

Enchanting Castle Apartments within a romantic Regency Castle of timeless charm, and a much-loved home. (Grade II* Listed Building of Architectural/Historic interest). Centrally situated in gentle Snowdonian foothills for enjoying North Wales' magnificent mountains, beaches, resorts, heritage and history. Many local restaurants and inns nearby. (Details available in our Information Room). A delightfully unique selection for 2-4 persons of fully self-contained, beautifully appointed, spacious, clean and peaceful accommodation, each with its own distinctive, individual character. Generously and graciously enhanced from antiques ... to dishwasher. 32 acres of truly tranquil landscaped gardens, sweeping lawns, woodland walks and panoramic hill-walk overlooking sea, Anglesey and Snowdon. The comfortable, warm and welcoming Castle in serene surroundings is open all year, including for short breaks, offering privacy and relaxation – ideal for couples. Regret children not accepted. Fully inclusive rents, including breakfast cereals etc., and much, much more...

Please contact Mrs Marita Gray-Parry directly any time for a brochure/booking
Self catering Apartments within the Castle
e.g. 2 persons for 2 nights from £195 incl "Romantic Breaks"

Anglesey & Gwynedd

North Wales

Ceredigion

THE Hafod Hotel

**Devil's Bridge,
Aberystwyth SY23 3JL
Tel: 01970 890232
Fax: 01970 890394**

Standing at the head of the Mynach Falls, perfect for exploring some of Wales' most spectacular scenery. Most bedrooms enjoy superb views. The restaurant offers a range of traditional fare, and there is a delightful Victorian Tea Room.

Within 20 min drive of Aberystwyth • Excellent food with a good selection of fine wines • Pets welcome • Superb walking country, with many circular walks from the doorstep • Fantastic birdwatching including Red Kites • Ideal for mountain biking and road biking.

• Family-owned and run.

**hafodhotel@btconnect.com
www.thehafodhotel.co.uk**

symbols

 Totally non-smoking

 Children Welcome

 Suitable for Disabled Guests

 Pets Welcome

 Christmas Breaks

 Licensed

Pembrokeshire

Powys

Oak Wood LODGES

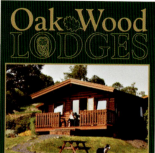

Llwynbaedd, Rhayader, Powys LD6 5NT

Luxurious Self Catering Log Cabins situated at approximately 1000ft above sea level with spectacular views of the Elan Valley and Cambrian mountains. Enjoy pursuits such as walking, pony trekking, mountain biking, fishing, and bird watching in the most idyllic of surroundings. Excellent touring centre. Dogs welcome. Short breaks as well as full weeks. Open all year round

For more information and brochure call:

01597 811422
www.oakwoodlodges.co.uk

Brynafon COUNTRY HOUSE HOTEL

South Street, Rhayader, Powys LD6 5BL
Tel: 01597 810735
e-mail: info@brynafon.co.uk • www.brynafon.co.uk

★★★

Once a workhouse and now a beautiful and very comfortable hotel, Brynafon has great character and charm. It is set against the dramatic backdrop of Gwastedyn Hill and the Druid's Circle, and is a stone's throw from the River Wye. Sitting in the very heart of the beautiful and still yet undiscovered Elan Valley, Brynafon is a must to visit any time of year. We cook fresh food each day, and change our set two and three-course menus five times per week, as well as offering a daily specials board. Our aim is to have a balanced menu which always has several vegetarian, meat and fish options. Brynafon has a total of 20 en suite bedrooms; three are family suites containing an extra bedroom, which brings the total number of bedrooms to 23. All are different, and most have beautiful views of the surrounding countryside.

B&B prices range from £61-£88 for two sharing, with family suites from £88. Brochure and tariff on request.

MADOG'S WELLS • Mid-Wales Holidays

Llanfair Caereinion, Welshpool, Powys SY21 0DE
Beautiful, peaceful valley with lots of wildlife.
Three bungalows, wheelchair accessible. Free gas, electricity and linen. Cot and iron also available on request. Games room and children's play area. Daily rates available out of main school holidays. Two three-bedroom bungalows (WTB ★★★★★) from £140 to £495. Two bedroom bungalow (WTB ★★★) £100 to £300. Open all year.

Contact Michael & Ann Reed for further details • Tel/Fax: 01938 810446
e-mail: info@madogswells.co.uk • www.madogswells.co.uk

South Wales

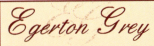

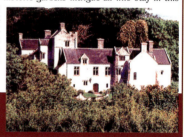

Ireland

photo supplied by Killarney Golf & Fishing Club, Killarney, Co Kerry.

A LAND OF HISTORY AND HERITAGE, myths and magic, Ireland is easily accessible by plane or ferry, and ideal for a Short Break holiday at any time of year.

Northern Ireland's beauty is intertwined with tragic history, rich culture and the renowned friendliness of its people. The wild craggy mountains, splendid lakes and sweeping coastline make it an ideal playground for watersports enthusiasts, walkers, cyclists, hikers, rock climbers and sailors. But there are lots of things to keep those after a dose of culture enthralled, too. From oyster festivals to authentic horse fairs, and from ancient castles to elegant country houses, this spectacular part of Ireland is packed with things to do.

From the endless attractions of Dublin with its lively nightlife, museums and art galleries and, of course, its literary connection with Swift, Shaw, Yeats, Joyce and Beckett, to the charming west of Ireland where genuine hospitality is part of the culture, there are plenty of things to do and places to visit. The south-east area is steeped in history and boasts a heritage trail unrivalled by any other region in Ireland. Cork and Kerry to the south are perhaps the most attractive holiday areas, with a long coastline, mountains, many rivers and lakes. Some of Ireland's finest heritage attractions are to be found in the eastern coastal and midlands region, including prehistoric monuments, Celtic monasteries, castles, and grand houses and gardens. But it's not all about action. There's plenty of opportunity to relax; perhaps to enjoy a peaceful cruise on the waterways, or a chat with the locals in one of the friendly pubs and, best of all, to experience the warmest of warm welcomes wherever you go.

Tourism Ireland
0800 039 7000
www.discoverireland.com

Why not Be Our Guest in Ireland?

Ireland

Index of Towns and Counties

BEKONSCOT MODEL VILLAGE & RAILWAY

Warwick Road, Beaconsfield,
Buckinghamshire HP9 2PL
Tel: 01494 672919
e-mail: info@bekonscot.co.uk
www.bekonscot.com

READERS' OFFER 2008

One child FREE when accompanied by full-paying adult
Valid February to October 2008

TAMAR VALLEY DONKEY PARK

St Ann's Chapel, Gunnislake,
Cornwall PL18 9HW
Tel: 01822 834072
e-mail: info@donkeypark.com
www.donkeypark.com

READERS' OFFER 2008

50p OFF per person, up to 6 persons
Valid from Easter until end October 2008

CARS OF THE STARS MOTOR MUSEUM

Standish Street, Keswick,
Cumbria CA12 5HH
Tel: 017687 73757
e-mail: cotsmm@aol.com
www.carsofthestars.com

READERS' OFFER 2008

One child free with two paying adults
Valid during 2008

WOODLANDS

Blackawton, Dartmouth,
Devon TQ9 7DQ
Tel: 01803 712598 • Fax: 01803 712680
e-mail: fun@woodlandspark.com
www.woodlandspark.com

READERS' OFFER 2008

12% discount off individual entry price for up to 4
persons. No photocopies. Valid 15/3/08 – 1/11/08

Be a giant in a magical miniature world of make-believe depicting rural England in the 1930s.
"A little piece of history that is forever England."

Open: 10am-5pm daily mid February to end October.

Directions: Junction 16 M25, Junction 2 M40.

Cornwall's only Donkey Sanctuary set in 14 acres overlooking the beautiful Tamar Valley. Donkey rides, rabbit warren, goat hill, children's playgrounds, cafe and picnic area. New all-weather play barn.

Open: Easter to end Oct: daily 10am to 5.30pm. Nov to March: weekends and all school holidays 10.30am to 4.30pm

Directions: just off A390 between Callington and Gunnislake at St Ann's Chapel.

A collection of cars from film and TV, including Chitty Chitty Bang Bang, James Bond's Aston Martin, Del Boy's van, Fab1 and many more.

PETS MUST BE KEPT ON LEAD

Open: daily 10am-5pm. Open February half term, 1st April to end November, also weekends in December.

Directions: in centre of Keswick close to car park.

All weather fun - guaranteed!
Unique combination of indoor/outdoor attractions. 3 Watercoasters, Toboggan Run, Arctic Gliders, boats, 15 Playzones for all ages. Biggest indoor venture zone in UK with 5 floors of play and rides. New Big Fun Farm with U-drive Tractor ride, Pedal Town and Yard Racers. Falconry Centre.

Open: mid-March to November open daily at 9.30am. Winter: open weekends and local school holidays.

Directions: 5 miles from Dartmouth on A3122. Follow brown tourist signs from A38.

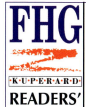

EXPLOSION! MUSEUM OF NAVAL FIREPOWER

Priddy's Hard, Gosport
Hampshire PO12 4LE
Tel: 023 9250 5600 • Fax: 023 9250 5605
e-mail: info@explosion.org.uk
www.explosion.org.uk

*SPECIAL OFFER 2008 - entry for just £1 per person.
One person per voucher. Not valid for events tickets.*

READERS' OFFER 2008

NOT TO BE USED IN CONJUNCTION WITH ANY OTHER OFFER

THE BEATLES STORY

Britannia Vaults, Albert Dock
Liverpool L3 4AD
Tel: 0151-709 1963 • Fax: 0151-708 0039
e-mail: info@beatlesstory.com
www.beatlesstory.com

*One FREE child with one full paying adult
Valid during 2008*

READERS' OFFER 2008

NOT TO BE USED IN CONJUNCTION WITH ANY OTHER OFFER

THE TALES OF ROBIN HOOD

30 - 38 Maid Marian Way,
Nottingham NG1 6GF
Tel: 0115 9483284 • Fax: 0115 9501536
e-mail: robinhoodcentre@mail.com
www.robinhood.uk.com

*One FREE child with full paying adult per voucher
Valid from January to December 2008*

READERS' OFFER 2008

NOT TO BE USED IN CONJUNCTION WITH ANY OTHER OFFER

WORLD OF JAMES HERRIOT

23 Kirkgate, Thirsk,
North Yorkshire YO7 1PL
Tel: 01845 524234
Fax: 01845 525333
www.worldofjamesherriot.org

*Admit TWO for the price of ONE (one voucher per
transaction only). Valid until October 2008*

READERS' OFFER 2008

NOT TO BE USED IN CONJUNCTION WITH ANY OTHER OFFER

A hands-on interactive museum, telling the story of naval warfare from gunpowder to modern missiles. Also fascinating social history of how 2500 women worked on the site during World War II. Gift shop and Waterside Coffee Shop with stunning harbour views.

Open: Saturday and Sunday 10am to 4pm (last entry one hour before closing).

Directions: M27 to J11, follow A32 to Gosport; signposted.
By rail to Portsmouth Harbour, then ferry to Gosport.

A unique visitor attraction that transports you on an enlightening and atmospheric journey into the life, times, culture and music of the Beatles. See how four young lads from Liverpool were propelled into the dizzy heights of worldwide fame and fortune to become the greatest band of all time. Hear the story unfold through the 'Living History' audio guide narrated by John Lennon's sister, Julia.

Open: daily 10am to 6pm (last admisssion 5pm) all year round (excl. 25/26 December)

Directions: located within Liverpool's historic Albert Dock.

Travel back in time with Robin Hood and his merry men on an adventure-packed theme tour, exploring the intriguing and mysterious story of their legendary tales of Medieval England. Enjoy film shows, live performances, adventure rides and even try archery! Are you brave enough to join Robin on his quest for good against evil?

Open: 10am-5.30pm, last admission 4.30pm.

Directions: follow the brown and white tourist information signs whilst heading towards the city centre.

Visit James Herriot's original house recreated as it was in the 1940s. Television sets used in the series 'All Creatures Great and Small'. There is a children's interactive gallery with life-size model farm animals and three rooms dedicated to the history of veterinary medicine.

Open: daily. Easter-Oct 10am-5pm; Nov-Easter 11am to 4pm

Directions: follow signs off A1 or A19 to Thirsk, then A168, off Thirsk market place

INVERARAY JAIL
Church Square, Inveraray,
Argyll PA32 8TX
Tel: 01499 302381• Fax: 01499 302195
e-mail: info@inverarayjail.co.uk
www.inverarayjail.co.uk

READERS'
OFFER
2008

> *One child FREE with one full-paying adult*
> *Valid until end 2008*

NOT TO BE USED IN CONJUNCTION WITH ANY OTHER OFFER

CREETOWN GEM ROCK MUSEUM
Chain Road, Creetown, Newton Stewart
Dumfries & Galloway DG8 7HJ
Tel: 01671 820357 • Fax: 01671 820554
e-mail: enquiries@gemrock.net
www.gemrock.net

READERS'
OFFER
2008

> *10% discount on admission.*
> *Valid during 2008.*

NOT TO BE USED IN CONJUNCTION WITH ANY OTHER OFFER

BO'NESS & KINNEIL RAILWAY
Bo'ness Station, Union Street,
Bo'ness, West Lothian EH51 9AQ
Tel: 01506 822298
e-mail: enquiries.railway@srps.org.uk
www.srps.org.uk

READERS'
OFFER
2008

> *FREE child train fare with one paying adult/concession. Valid 29th*
> *March-26th Oct 2008. Not Thomas events or Santa Steam trains*

NOT TO BE USED IN CONJUNCTION WITH ANY OTHER OFFER

CLYDEBUILT SCOTTISH MARITIME MUSEUM
Braehead Shopping Centre, King's Inch Road,
Glasgow G51 4BN

Tel: 0141-886 1013 • Fax: 0141-886 1015
e-mail: clydebuilt@scotmaritime.org.uk
www.scottishmaritimemuseum.org

READERS'
OFFER
2008

> *HALF PRICE admission for up to 4 persons.*
> *Valid during 2008.*

NOT TO BE USED IN CONJUNCTION WITH ANY OTHER OFFER

204

19th century prison with fully restored 1820 courtroom and two prisons. Guides in uniform as warders, prisoners and matron. Remember your camera!

Open: April to October 9.30am-6pm (last admission 5pm); November to March 10am-5pm (last admission 4pm)

Directions: A83 to Campbeltown

A fantastic display of gems, crystals, minerals and fossils. An experience you'll treasure forever. Gift shop, tearoom and AV display.

Open: Summer - 9.30am to 5.30pm daily; Winter - 10am to 4pm daily. Closed Christmas to end January.

Directions: follow signs from A75 Dumfries/Stranraer.

Steam and heritage diesel passenger trains from Bo'ness to Birkhill for guided tours of Birkhill fireclay mines. Explore the history of Scotland's railways in the Scottish Railway Exhibition. Coffee shop and souvenir shop.

Open: weekends Easter to October, daily July and August.

Directions: in the town of Bo'ness. Leave M9 at Junction 3 or 5, then follow brown tourist signs.

The story of Glasgow and the River Clyde brought vividly to life using AV, hands-on and interactive techniques. You can navigate your own ship, safely load your cargo, operate an engine, and go aboard the 130-year-old coaster 'Kyles'. Ideal for kids young and old wanting an exciting day out. New - The Clyde's Navy.

Open: 10am to 5.30pm daily

Directions: Green Car Park near M&S at Braehead Shopping Centre.

LLANBERIS LAKE RAILWAY
Gilfach Ddu, Llanberis,
Gwynedd LL55 4TY
Tel: 01286 870549
e-mail: info@lake-railway.co.uk
www.lake-railway.co.uk

*One pet travels FREE with each full fare paying adult
Valid Easter to October 2008*

NOT TO BE USED IN CONJUNCTION WITH ANY OTHER OFFER

FELINWYNT RAINFOREST CENTRE
Felinwynt, Cardigan,
Ceredigion SA43 1RT
Tel: 01239 810882/810250
e-mail: dandjdevereux@btinternet.com
www.butterflycentre.co.uk

*TWO for the price of ONE (one voucher per party only)
Valid until end October 2008*

NOT TO BE USED IN CONJUNCTION WITH ANY OTHER OFFER

NATIONAL CYCLE COLLECTION
Automobile Palace, Temple Street,
Llandrindod Wells, Powys LD1 5DL
Tel: 01597 825531
e-mail: cycle.museum@powys.org.uk
www.cyclemuseum.org.uk

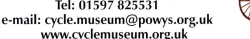

*TWO for the price of ONE
Valid during 2008 except Special Event days*

NOT TO BE USED IN CONJUNCTION WITH ANY OTHER OFFER

RHONDDA HERITAGE PARK
Lewis Merthyr Colliery, Coed Cae Road,
Trehafod, Near Pontypridd CF37 2NP
Tel: 01443 682036
e-mail: info@rhonddaheritagepark.com
www.rhonddaheritagepark.com

*Two adults or children for the price of one when accompanied
by a full paying adult. Valid until end 2008 for full tours only.
Not valid on special event days/themed tours.*

NOT TO BE USED IN CONJUNCTION WITH ANY OTHER OFFER

A 60-minute ride along the shores of beautiful Padarn Lake behind a quaint historic steam engine. Magnificent views of the mountains from lakeside picnic spots.

DOGS MUST BE KEPT ON LEAD AT ALL TIMES ON TRAIN

Open: most days Easter to October. Free timetable leaflet on request.

Directions: just off A4086 Caernarfon to Capel Curig road at Llanberis; follow 'Country Park' signs.

Mini-rainforest full of tropical plants and exotic butterflies. Personal attention of the owner, Mr John Devereux. Gift shop, cafe, video room, exhibition. Suitable for disabled visitors. VisitWales Quality Assured Visitor Attraction.

PETS NOT ALLOWED IN TROPICAL HOUSE ONLY

Open: daily Easter to end October 10.30am to 5pm

Directions: West Wales, 7 miles north of Cardigan off Aberystwyth road. Follow brown tourist signs on A487.

Journey through the lanes of cycle history and see bicycles from Boneshakers and Penny Farthings up to modern Raleigh cycles. Over 250 machines on display

PETS MUST BE KEPT ON LEADS

Open: 1st March to 1st November daily 10am onwards.

Directions: brown signs to car park. Town centre attraction.

Make a pit stop whatever the weather! Join an ex-miner on a tour of discovery, ride the cage to pit bottom and take a thrilling ride back to the surface. Multi-media presentations, period village street, children's adventure play area, restaurant and gift shop. Disabled access with assistance.

Open: Open daily 10am to 6pm (last tour 4pm). Closed Mondays Oct - Easter, also Dec 25th to early Jan.

Directions: Exit Junction 32 M4, signposted from A470 Pontypridd. Trehafod is located between Pontypridd and Porth.

FHG Guides Ltd have a large range of attractive holiday accommodation guides for all kinds of holiday opportunities throughout Britain. They also make useful gifts at any time of year.
Our guides are available in most bookshops and larger newsagents but we will be happy to post you a copy direct if you have any difficulty. POST FREE for addresses in the UK.
We will also post abroad but have to charge separately for post or freight.

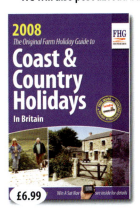

The original Farm Holiday Guide to COAST & COUNTRY HOLIDAYS in England, Scotland, Wales and Channel Islands. Board, Self-catering, Caravans/Camping, Activity Holidays.

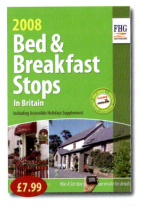

BED AND BREAKFAST STOPS Over 1000 friendly and comfortable overnight stops. Non-smoking, Disabled and Special Diets Supplements.

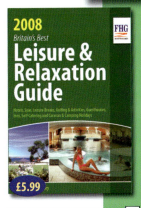

BRITAIN'S BEST LEISURE & RELAXATION GUIDE A quick-reference general guide for all kinds of holidays.

The Original PETS WELCOME! The bestselling guide to holidays for pet owners and their pets.

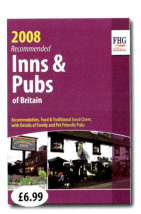

Recommended INNS & PUBS of Britain Including Pubs, Inns and Small Hotels.

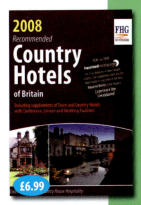

Recommended COUNTRY HOTELS of Britain Including Country Houses for the discriminating.

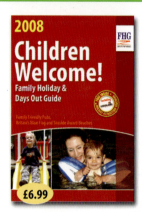

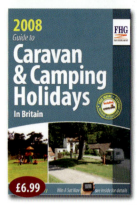

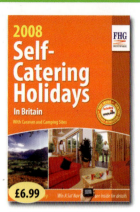

CHILDREN WELCOME! Family Holidays and Days Out guide.
Family holidays with details of amenities for children and babies.

The FHG Guide to CARAVAN & CAMPING HOLIDAYS
Caravans for hire, sites and holiday parks and centres.

SELF-CATERING HOLIDAYS in Britain
Over 1000 addresses throughout for self-catering and caravans in Britain.

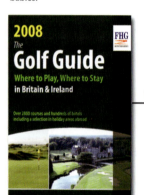

The GOLF GUIDE – *Where to play Where to stay*
In association with GOLF MONTHLY. Over 2800 golf courses in Britain with convenient accommodation. Holiday Golf in France, Portugal, Spain, USA and Thailand.

£9.99

Tick your choice above and send your order and payment to

FHG Guides Ltd. Abbey Mill Business Centre
Seedhill, Paisley, Scotland PA1 1TJ
TEL: 0141- 887 0428 • FAX: 0141- 889 7204
e-mail: admin@fhguides.co.uk

Deduct 10% for 2/3 titles or copies; 20% for 4 or more.

Send to: NAME ....

ADDRESS ....

....

....

POST CODE ....

I enclose Cheque/Postal Order for £ ....

SIGNATURE ....DATE ....

Please complete the following to help us improve the service we provide.

How did you find out about our guides?:

☐ Press   ☐ Magazines   ☐ TV/Radio   ☐ Family/Friend   ☐ Other